Sandy Farrell

526-9324

Also by John T. Kirk

AMERICAN CHAIRS: QUEEN ANNE AND CHIPPENDALE
1972

EARLY AMERICAN FURNITURE
1970

CONNECTICUT FURNITURE,
SEVENTEENTH AND EIGHTEENTH CENTURIES
1967

THE
IMPECUNIOUS
COLLECTOR'S
GUIDE TO
AMERICAN
ANTIQUES

What early American furniture and other objects can still be found at modest prices.

How to recognize if a piece is genuine and has permanent aesthetic merit.

How to spot something good in a cluttered shop.

How to buy it without paying too much.

How to display it to best advantage.

THE IMPECUNIOUS COLLECTOR'S GUIDE TO AMERICAN ANTIQUES

JOHN T. KIRK

ALFRED A. KNOPF   NEW YORK   1980

THIS IS A BORZOI BOOK
PUBLISHED BY ALFRED A. KNOPF, INC.

Copyright © 1975 by John T. Kirk
All rights reserved under International and Pan-American Copyright Conventions.
Published in the United States by Alfred A. Knopf, Inc., New York,
and simultaneously in Canada by Random House of Canada Limited, Toronto.
Distributed by Random House, Inc., New York.

Library of Congress Cataloging in Publication Data

Kirk, John T.   The impecunious collector's guide to early American antiques.

1. Art industries and trade, Early American—Collectors and collecting. I. Title.
NK806.K5   745.1'0973   75–8224
ISBN 0–394–49620–5
ISBN 0–394–73096–8 pbk.

Manufactured in the United States of America
Published November 18, 1975
Reprinted Twice
Fourth Printing, September 1980

To Elizabeth H. Kirk and Samuel E. Kirk

"To have some discernment of beauty is no less essential to man than to possess the attributes of speech and reason. . . . Taste is certainly not an arbitrary principle, which is subject to the fancy of every individual, and which admits of no criterion for determining whether it be true or false."

—HUGH BLAIR, D.D., 1825

Contents

Acknowledgments

It is impossible to thank by name all those who have helped with a book like this. Many have done so with a passing word, phrase, or idea which I have long incorporated into my thinking, forgetting it was not my invention. Others have helped by saying things that made me realize I thought the opposite. As always I am indebted to the early writers who loved and wrote about furniture. Now they are castigated for what they did not do, or did wrong, or said or did not say; we will have a similar turn. But above all I want to thank the objects for being. Perhaps I should thank the makers and purchasers who caused them, yet their actions involved money and ego, while the objects did not know this, so I praise them.

Philip and Helen Greven's flinching at what I consider great surfaces helped me to see that everyone is not as enamored of character as I, thus making me try to present my thoughts and feelings clearly. Syrl Silberman's "What's a Hitchcock chair? I don't know and I'm no dummy," helped me realize the importance of taking nothing for granted. Benno Forman has joyously pierced balloons while inflating others. Derek Shrub, Michael Fay, and David Jewell have encouraged joyous irreverence. Rigmore Andersen and Meyric Rogers must always be mentioned, since they helped me to see.

Charles Montgomery helped in various ways with Yale's pieces. Pat Kane made it possible to take fewer trips to Yale by supplying photographs and information. Jonathan Fairbanks made material available at the Museum of Fine Arts, and Ann Farnam helped with photographs and information from there. Henry Harlow provided information and pictures from Sturbridge, and Jackie Oak material from Shelburne. Ruth and Roger Bacon's enthusiasm for an interesting piece even if it lacks a leg or is full of holes has reinforced my similar attitude. Albert Sack and Harold Sack have made objects available for study and provided photographs. Mr. and Mrs. John Wright discussed why they buy American furniture and how they do so inexpensively. Ted Benfey first showed me the many facets of Pooh.

Jane Garrett as editor encouraged a freewheeling manuscript, and Ellen Neuwald helped Knopf to view it enthusiastically. The Robbins, Genie and Danny, provided Farcival Farm, where the outline for this book developed amidst melting snow and bulging fires. Dick Benjamin produced many of the photographs that made it possible to see the pieces. Frieda Place has once again cheerfully struggled with endless tapes and messy pages.

Elizabeth D. Kirk encouraged and shared a growing interest in inexpensive pieces of exciting quality and character, and she pushed for an outline and manuscript that would reflect a joyous delight "in revealing their pleasures." Trevor Fairbrother, during cold and heat, helped revise the outline and manuscript. His typing, editing, and discussion of the photographs and objects has brought about much of what clarity exists.

This book is dedicated to my parents, who placed first the education of their children. They made possible an unusual range of training and experiences, and I am grateful. And then there is Natasha, who leaves the room when anything phony, plastic, or chrome enters. I do not know if she has a great eye, or a great nose, for quality.

John T. Kirk
Daniel Bliss House
1975

Introduction

This book is a response to friends, beginning collectors, advanced collectors, and all those just casually interested in American furniture who ask: "What is there worth buying at a price I can afford? How do I know I should buy it? How do I know it is okay to buy it? How *do* I buy it— the whole process, the dealers, the auctions, the fakes? What do I believe? Who do I believe? Which dealer do I believe? What kind of risk am I taking? Are there ways that I can go about selecting, buying, and paying for an object which will give me some sense of having spent my money without wasting it? It is not just that a piece might turn out to be something different than it is purported to be; even if it is genuine, how will I know that I will like it in six months, or a year, or six years? Is there such a thing as a piece that will *always* be excellent, or do tastes and ideas about furniture and other objects, and design in general, just change? How do I know that next year, or ten years from now, it will be considered a good design?"

All this includes whether a piece is a fake, or is being sold as American when it is English, Portuguese, or Scandinavian. So there are really two things to learn: how to recognize what a genuine object should look like, and how to choose from among the genuine the one which has permanent aesthetic merit. The first demands exacting knowledge that must expand as unscrupulous dealers learn more sophisticated faking techniques and of new sources for foreign objects that can be sold as American. For the second, one must always be aware that a genuine piece is not necessarily beautiful since there were thousands of mediocre designer-cabinetmakers.

I hope this book will make the average weekend seeker after Americana, those thousands who drive the roads in hope of finding a junk shop with a masterpiece, more able to discriminate between the junk of which there is so much and the relatively inexpensive marvelous. I hope to stretch the imagination and train the eye to comparison and judgment about objects, while realizing the subjectivity of such a process.

This book presents in words and photographs

1. *Desk and bookcase. Rhode Island, Newport. 1755–1795. Made by the Goddard and Townsend families. Courtesy, Museum of Fine Arts, Boston; M. and M. Karolik Collection.*

the problems of perceiving an object, although this can only be fully experienced by a personal confrontation with real pieces. It describes the process of perception, of coming to grips with what is in front of your nose, whether what is there is early or modern. It deals with how one comes to love or hate a piece. The word "love" does apply to a relationship with an object if it is truly great, if it is a piece with which one has a new and continually renewed, often long-lasting relationship; and a fake can certainly be hated. A genuine piece that is second-, third-, fourth-, or even tenth-rate probably does not deserve to be hated, but it should be set apart and to a great degree ignored; it can be enjoyed for showing how bad the early cabinetmakers could be, or it can be used comparatively to reveal the extraordinary quality of a fine piece. We are surrounded by devastatingly uninteresting things from every period and most of what we see is junk and should be discarded as such. Many who like early things think that nothing made recently is worth looking at, but I am referring to things from all times, periods, and styles and not just to early pieces. Great new forms, some of the most beautiful things ever made, are being created right now.

This book is not a sequential survey of American pieces from the first years to the present, nor is it an attempt to provide endless photographs against which seekers can compare a find. Indeed, it would be impossible to produce such a book; an extended series would be necessary, and even then the next object would be different from any of those pictured. I have, therefore, used a selected group of objects by which I can describe the process of learning to judge, perceive, and appreciate or dislike a piece. If you learn an openness, an awareness, if you train your eye to finer and finer perception of mass, line, all-over final statement, and surface texture, you can approach anything ancient or modern, man-made or natural. It is the way of perceiving, of being vulnerable while maintaining the most stringently demanding, aggressively demanding, criteria for excellence.

I want to make it absolutely clear at the beginning that a piece deserving of appreciation and praise need not be an elaborate, expensive, high-style (sophisticated urban-made) piece. In fact, I can more easily, more quickly love a piece like the hanging cupboard, figure 2, than I can the superbly organized desk and bookcase made by the Goddard and Townsend families in Newport, Rhode Island, figure 1. The latter is hard to get to know, while the cupboard is immediately available to the viewer. It is simply boards nailed together and covered with a direct surface design of dark red paint enriched by diagonally arranged white polka dots; the whole has been worn and battered to a deliciously grungy surface that is now both personal and intriguing. The bookcase on desk is different; this takes much more work to understand than the cupboard, since it openly demands more. It must be approached intellectually as well as emotionally, for it has the finest organization created during the best hours of one of the superb cabinetmakers in a great design center. A greater designer put more there to be perceived. While figure 2 allows immediate enjoyment of form and pattern, figure 1 demands the ultimate involvement of mind, body, and soul. Also, developed high-style pieces like figure 1 must be *absolutely* first-rate in every way since a second-rate version is awful, while primitive pieces have many ways in which to be wonderful: shape, color, patterned enrichment, surface. Although these two pieces seem worlds apart, it should be realized that they are similar in their attempt to satisfy a desire for enriched, highly patterned objects that would intrigue the eye and enliven the environment. These two pieces are much closer to each other than either is to stripped-to-essentials modern.

2. *Hanging cupboard. New England; found installed in an early house near Exeter, New Hampshire. Early nineteenth century. Seen also in figure 89. Privately owned.*

My intention, then, is to verbalize one approach to objects. There are, of course, other approaches, but for me it is basically a question of quality of design: the judging between one thing and another, one and many, one and most. After publishing an earlier book, which dealt with the proportions of the more elaborate early furniture and mentioned the importance of early painted surfaces, I received two letters that I have thought about as I worked on this book. The first writer said that she had always seen furniture as chiefly the use of varying proportions, but her friends thought she was silly; the second writer loved old surfaces but friends kept asking when the pieces were going to be cleaned up, "refinished," and it had been hard to resist their pressure. This book is, in part, a reaction to such "friends," for it is about the art of looking: perceiving and understanding what is there to be seen, not what you can do to a piece. It investigates the art of being vulnerable to quality and demanding it.

THE
IMPECUNIOUS
COLLECTOR'S
GUIDE TO
AMERICAN
ANTIQUES

1

Perception Without Prejudice

PREJUDICES

Most of us want an object to walk out and talk to us, to appeal directly without our having to work at seeing it; this includes our asking the same thing of all pieces, that they fit our preconceived ideas of what a piece should be. In this way we miss seeing great things with which we are unfamiliar. Every period, whether we like its style or not, produced great designs. There are those who loathe the mid-nineteenth-century Victorian rococo revival, and those who hate the early-twentieth-century work of the Bauhaus—those rectilinear, hard-lined, consciously functional objects. But while our responsibility is not to like all styles, it is to perceive and understand the best that each produced. We may find, if we work at it, that we have ignored many styles and tastes in design that will appeal to us, and we may even come to like them, once we understand them, and those we learn to like may be easier and cheaper to obtain.

For a piece to be properly perceived, it must first be considered in terms of what it was meant to be—its basic concept and what made it look the way it does. And, initially it must be judged against its peers, not against pieces from other styles and dates. For example, it is not fair to take a very early object and demand of it all that we like in modern ones. We cannot expect an early-eighteenth-century chair to be comfortable by modern standards, for comfort as we know it had not been invented. Chairs made about 1700 *are* miserably uncomfortable; if you demand comfort, then you should collect objects that were made after comfort became a factor in design. The first responsibility of a great object is to reach an aesthetic level superior to most of the similar pieces made at the same time. Only then can it be compared to similarly great forms from other historic periods. If we can approach an object in terms of what *it* was attempting to do, what *its* designer-maker wanted to communicate to its original viewers, we may find it superior and exciting even though we still do not "like" it. The phrase "I wouldn't want to live with it" is common, but no one is asking anyone to live with everything. Perception without prejudice enables us to enjoy many things with which we have no intention of living.

THE DECORATOR'S ATTITUDE

The person who strides into an antique shop with a piece of knotted string, saying, "I have this much space between two windows," is asking for trouble. So is the person bearing a piece of chintz, velvet, or damask, and wanting "something to go with it." This is like ordering a Cézanne to fit a given space or to go with the decor, instead of buying a *great* Cézanne and changing the decor to go with it. And it is asking to be shown something that the dealer has been dying to get rid of, or has kept aside for just such a customer. In an expensive shop, such pieces are known as "trade goods." A related and equally inadequate approach is made by the person who wants to do up a room in the "Chippendale" or "Queen Anne" style. To go looking for objects in these ways not only encourages the dealer to pass off something inadequate; it also means closing your eyes to the wonderful things that you may encounter. The great objects are so few, so hard to find, and often so difficult to afford when you do find them that you should buy them if you can, and *then* a space should be found for them. If they are truly wonderful, you will make room.

WANT-LISTS

Another limiting but common approach is to take the main volumes on American furniture and list the kinds of pieces you want: a "butterfly" table, a splay-leg "tavern" table, a slat-back chair, a Windsor chair, a bannister-back chair, and so on. Usually these are now the scarce forms, and in some instances they were rare at the time they were created. Some forms were made in quantity—slat backs and Windsors, for example—but list-makers usually note only the rarest and earliest types of these. For such customers, some dealers will cheerfully create what is sought; and, as with the chintz-bearers, these buyers cut themselves off from the more common forms that might be better designed, as well as cheaper, than what is left of the genuine rare forms.

Lists put blinders on collectors so that they may reach for the rare but inadequate while missing something else that they have never learned to see, or never known they should look at. I would rather have a simple, well-designed, and untouched nineteenth-century slat-back chair like figure 3 than one like the earlier but restored and skinned figure 4. What has happened to figure 4 should not happen to any chair, for it is now not old—it is the *inside* of the original chair. The paint and the original wood surface are gone; both have been thrown on the floor with the sandpaper. An old surface is what makes an early piece different from a good copy: the color and patina are so thin that in sanding you soon reveal the nasty bright yellow of fresh-cut maple. The top two-thirds of the finials of this arm chair are new, but you cannot see this for they are in surface and color just like the raw "new maple" of the back posts. The novice with a list might well miss figure 3 while getting excited over the rarer features of figure 4, its fancier shaping and turnings.

Acquaintance with the literature of the field is essential, but one cannot expect to use furniture books like a Sears catalogue. Anyone who thinks that, guarded only by a little book knowledge, he can trip through the antique shops and find great treasures is a fool. There never were that many good pieces, and now there are fewer; seldom are they found lying around at a low price. It takes work and knowledge to find anything worth buying.

3. *Side chair. New England; found in central New Hampshire. Nineteenth century. Privately owned.*

4. *Arm chair. New England. 1780–1820. Courtesy, Knut Ek.*

UNIQUENESS

Another attitude that cripples collectors, and one related to list-making, is the demand for uniqueness: the William and Mary (1700–1735) highboy with no drawers in the base or stand, when usually they have one to four; the four- or five-legged William and Mary highboy, when usually they have six, four across the front; the art glass of certain colors and patterns; the documented piece; and so forth. What does it matter if you have the only one with such-and-such an inlay, with one more do-dad than on the related

piece at the Metropolitan Museum, or that your chest of drawers is the only one of that form known whose top has rounded front corners? It may be that such a rare piece *is* the highest development by a great artist; it may also be a clumsy exception by a good designer, or the work of an inept maker, or just a fake. One should ask, "If this was made at a certain time and found to be successful, why aren't there others?" Seeking only the rare brings out the best in the fakers and the worst in collectors for it gives them, like the list-makers, blinders. All these attitudes are like ordering a steak from a red rather than a black cow, instead of ordering a great steak. Anyone wishing to buy wonderful things must get beyond the "stamp-collecting attitude." Now I know that stamp collectors will write irate letters condemning this comparison, but I turn away from prizing something because the airplane is upside down. To make such a mistake interesting, I would want the plane's reversal to have produced a new aesthetic experience, not just a unique one.

The real "why" of collecting lies in the ability to be in contact with and relate to beauty, and that does not depend on uniqueness; it depends on how a piece looks now, what makes it available to you, and what it does to you. Often, with the pieces seen here, it is not how they originally looked that makes their greatness or impact, but what has happened to them: through aging many have arrived at a unique and wonderful personality.

PRICE: FINDING THE INEXPENSIVE

A basic problem is how much you should spend. Since thinking in terms of investment can easily warp one's perception and judgment, probably beginning collectors, or even somewhat advanced ones, should spend only the amount that they can afford to waste or to pay for new objects. Obviously, this could range between $5.00 and $5,000. Maybe it should be judged by what one can afford to spend on an evening's entertainment, or a vacation.

It is, of course, possible to buy items from categories that are not yet expensive, and that would be the best and quickest way to buy cheaply. But if you are trying to buy inexpensively items in categories already bordering on or within the expensive range, then the only solution is to go where their value, aesthetic and monetary, is not understood. A collector needs either time or money. Some of both is helpful,

but lots of one will drastically reduce the need for the other. Almost as much as knowledge, the impecunious collector needs the capacity to enjoy going to the sort of shop where virtually everything is worthless, and where it will be difficult to find anything exciting. The impecunious collector will often find the appropriateness of a shop to be in direct proportion to the unpleasantness of its smell. Recently I purchased for a museum house a fine eighteenth-century washstand in a shop that was difficult to enter because of the clutter and an atmosphere which made seeing almost impossible. You had to squint your eyes against the smarting effect of unhousebroken puppy united with cheap, perfumed "room freshener." Fortunately, it was possible to take the stand outside for study, and a top-quality piece was purchased cheaply.

One reason prices are high is that dealers spend much of their time buying back and forth from each other, normally increasing the price at each sale. So you must get to the start of the chain by being willing to go where the most insignificant dealers go, to the smelliest and grungiest places. It is also a question of looking for things where they should not be. A great Victorian table can be priced at nothing in a fine shop that specializes in primitives, and a fine primitive may be well under-priced in a shop that carries mostly American and English high-style objects, or in a glass and china shop. Figure 5 was recently found considerably under-priced in such a shop, where it was displaying a "desirable" wash set. Had it been in a shop specializing in painted primitives, where its delightful painted "tiger maple" pattern was appreciated as rare and exciting, the price would have been very different. Figure 54 was found in a similar shop, painted with Chinese red enamel, draped in oilcloth, and stacked with poor-quality bits and pieces.

I was once on the lecture platform with

Abbott Lowell Cummings, the authority on early New England houses, talking about collecting and finding things; we faced an audience composed mostly of ladies, half of whom sported white gloves, while the other half were in sneakers. Cummings was explaining how to discover whether an unrestored early house was good or just ordinary. He stressed the significance of original fireplaces, and said, when only one is open, "Climb up its flue and down another flue, and look around with a flashlight." The same willingness to explore must be present in any collector trying for a find.

What Cummings meant is that dedication—complete commitment and its inherent personal cost—is the first step if one is going to be seriously involved in anything important. If impecunious collectors can enjoy "wasting" time, bear distaste in the process, and trust their own eyes and knowledge to gamble within their financial circumstances, they can build collections for perhaps one-tenth to one-quarter of the top "market value." They must, however, be willing to go to shops that make you want to wash your hands every time you touch something, as well as to auctions where most people will be waiting for the lawnmowers, the hide-a-beds, and the carnival glass.

It is unrealistic to talk as if antiques have a "retail price." The price is in direct proportion to the likelihood of its being recognized, understood, and afforded by the particular clientele of a given shop in a given area. It is true that many dealers who recognize something as great and know that their clients either will not appreciate it or cannot afford it will call another who deals in such items. But there is still a hope among all collectors that they will stumble across a "sleeper"—the term for a piece which a dealer does not understand and has not priced highly enough for its quality and rarity. It is said in the trade that every shop has its sleeper; if the col-

5. *Wash stand. New England. Knobs replaced. 1800–1840. Privately owned.*

6. Glass bowls. Left American, found in Rhode Island. Nineteenth century. Center and right (seen also in figure 87), English. Nineteenth century. Privately owned.

lector has sufficient grasp of design and knowledge of form and also knows to look out for the unexpected, he or she may make a great buy.

The bowl at the left of figure 6 was being auctioned as part of a lot, a group of things that had belonged to an early-twentieth-century dentist. It sat, almost full of ashes, among the extracting and drilling equipment which flanked the early dentist chair. The bowl was a mess; the ashes and dirt hid any quality of glass, or line of form. A snoopy collector picked it up and saw the pontil mark on its base that identified it as hand-blown. Looking hard at the *form*, he saw it to be interesting and asked the auctioneer to sell it separately. The auctioneer said, "But it's Pyrex." The collector insisted that he would only be a sure bidder if the bowl were isolated from the lot. It was, and he purchased it at a low price. No one else recognized it in its filthy state and inappropriate surroundings as a rare nineteenth-century piece. Even the auctioneer missed it, for he was thinking of dentistry when he said "Pyrex," instead of looking at the bowl. The other two glass bowls in figure 6 demonstrate a different but related problem. They were purchased in London and are English; but their light green-blue color would allow them to be sold as "Jersey" in an American shop.

FAKES

A buyer should be aware that when a piece is priced below its recognized market value in a shop where the owner knows that kind of object, it is a sign that something may be wrong—that the piece may not be a sleeper but either a fake or heavily restored. A low price is one of the quickest ways to get rid of an inadequate piece. Another is to place a fake where you would least expect to find it: in a house auction that pretends to be a sale of that house's contents (as we shall see in a later chapter) or in an early house occupied by an aged person. This is usually only worthwhile for expensive pieces, but a tottering Mrs. Brown in an early Newport house, with tears in her eyes, can easily pass off a well-faked "Rhode Island" piece, and her cut from the deal will help ward off those blustery New England winds.

Any collector who thinks he is duping a dealer should be aware that most dealers know more and have had more experience than most collectors. True, even in recent years, finds have been made; very expensive items bought cheaply because the buyer knew what he was doing and the dealer did not. But to do so, a buyer would have to perceive high quality in something the dealer thought rather standard, or know that a piece was of a different period than the dealer thought: perhaps that it was colonial instead of a later revival version, or that it was American when it was being sold as foreign. We should remember, however, that fake pieces—ones that are made "rarer," "more interesting," by having features added or removed—are dribbled before us on a seemingly daily schedule.

Some years ago, when I was putting together a show of Connecticut furniture at the Wadsworth Atheneum, I saw in an important shop a highboy covered with carved enrichment, and I asked for a photograph. While working with all the photographs I had gathered from many sources, I found that this elaborate piece seemed to be a link between two schools of Connecticut cabinetwork, for it had the basic form and some enrichment of one school although most of its decoration was from another. Intrigued, I returned to study the piece in detail and found that all the enrichment typical of the second school of workers was new. In "faking up" this piece to make it more elaborate the fakers had taken ideas from the wrong source. Years earlier, when elaborate Connecticut pieces were not as "collectable" the opposite happened: many elaborate ones were simplified, decoration removed, to suit the then more conservative buyers.

There is an early collector's story of a lady hunting antiques who, driving through northern New England, saw a wagonload of mediocre, late objects on which was perched a butterfly table—a rare, early form of dropleaf table, usually small in size. These have always been scarce and "very collectable." They would go on anybody's wantlist. The collector stopped the wagon driver and asked to buy certain items from among the mediocre, then said, "How about the little table on top?" The wagon driver said, "No, that is promised to my daughter." Increasing prices were mentioned, but again and again the driver declined. The price went up until the driver finally said, "Well, if you want it that much, I'll just have to give my daughter something else." And so the collector bought the only fake on the wagon, another victim of the wagon driver's ritualistic drive. Scoundrels can be very wise. Indeed "scoundrel" is not the correct word, for they are thieves.

You may think that you will not worry if a piece turns out to be different from what you thought it was; you may pride yourself on saying, "Well, if I love it now and it turns out to be a fake, I'll still love it; I mean, after all, I like it now, don't I?" But you will find that you are annoyed, pestered, and very upset by the price you paid, and by the actual event of buying it, until finally you get rid of the piece. You will say to yourself and, if you are honest, to anybody who comes into the room, "I know it's not the best but I love it," or, "I know there are some things wrong with it, but isn't it charming?" or, "I bought that before I knew as much as I know now" (which is of course true since you now know it to be a fake). You will also begin to realize that there are things about your piece that always bothered you, for a faker will without realizing it instill into a piece some element of his own period's consciousness. It is virtually impossible to make a colonial object today even if you make an "exact copy," for some facet of the time of manufacture is always there. People who made colonial revival objects in the late nineteenth and early twentieth centuries were often

7. Arm chair. Official chair of Brown University. Modern. Courtesy, Brown University Alumni office.

sure that they were being faithful in reproducing artifacts of earlier times; now we can see what they added, which stands out as different from *our* idea of the colonial.

MISUSE OF EARLY DESIGNS

One reason that we have difficulty in being selective, in getting ourselves to the point where we can understand the differences between the good, mediocre, and poor, is that we are surrounded by mediocrity—it is ubiquitous. Some years ago, my wife and I purchased a house built in 1714 in Orange, Connecticut. We asked the owner, who had loved the house but whose husband had found it too much work, what they had bought instead, for they were moving only a mile away. She said, "Neo-Howard Johnson's." We are surrounded by neo-Howard Johnson's: picture windows made up of tiny little panes of glass difficult to wash, impossible to see through, and as foreign to eighteenth-century houses as banana splits; wagon-wheel chandeliers; rifles posing as standing lamps; and aluminum pedestal bar stools with maple "Windsor" tops. We have created colonial *kitsch*, thinking it reflects our past. We accept it because we have been told that it is good, proper, and us.

When Brown University decided that it needed an official University chair, the alumni office, being deeply concerned that the chair should be representative of the University and Rhode Island taste at the time of its founding in 1764, set out to find what would be appropriate. A member of their staff visited museums and historic houses, consulted books and collectors, and corresponded with at least one of the leading New York dealers. Finally, he settled on a chair like the one in figure 8, which was the right date and had a Rhode Island history, and the dealer gave him permission to copy it. The chair is a high-quality, bow-back Windsor arm chair with mahogany arms and beautiful turnings. The alumni office then wrote to various modern chair-making firms and eventually forwarded the photograph to one that was to make the chair. In return, the firm suggested several alternative types which they felt would appropriately reflect the Rhode Island Windsor. They said they had a chair in production that was close to the one shown in the picture, but they suggested using another that they made as it was more suitable for modern use, being more comfortable and sturdy. It seems that at that point the alumni office which had worked so hard over a long period of time to understand what was "Rhode Island" and "quality" in a Windsor allowed the "more suitable" one, figure 7, to become the official University chair. A chair already in production had the Brown University seal affixed to the top or crest rail.

What is figure 7? It is not like figure 8. Although both have the shape of their legs repeated in the front turnings under the arms, here the similarity stops. On figure 8 that baluster shape is carried around the spokes of the back. The rhythm of these rayed spokes is enclosed by a sweeping crest rail that begins and ends in the seat, and the principal spokes are played against the two bracing spokes supported by a tongue projecting from the rear of the seat. There are three stretchers, two side and one medial. There is a saddle seat, carved to a sharp front edge that makes it look light; it is shaped to rise to a point at the center. The entire chair, except for the mahogany arms, is painted black. Those are the physical aspects, a description of the parts employed to make a design. But how were they used, what effect do they have on the viewer, early or modern? There is an airy, open feeling. The play of the balusters, one against another in different parts of the chair, provides a counterpoint, an interest that keeps the eye moving from one place to the next. The interplay of the two raking bracing spokes against the

8. *Arm chair. Probably Rhode Island. 1750–1800. Courtesy, Israel Sack, Inc., New York City.*

9. Arm chair. Probably New England. 1750–1800. Courtesy, The Henry Ford Museum, Dearborn, Michigan.

more vertical spokes of the back creates continuous eye entertainment, for the design never rests: as you walk across in front there is a changing play of spokes against spokes, angles against angles. It is slender, integrated, and elegant. This chair—and its kind—is one of the strong, original, and beautiful expressions in American design.

Figure 7 is very different. It is a thickly complex, squat, and unhappy design. One of the most unfortunate additions, certainly not typical of eighteenth-century work, is the stretcher between the back legs. This complicates the base, and the additional bracing it provides is unnecessary. The back is squashed down and fattened sideways. It looks as if it had been on a diet of beer and bananas. In proportion it is nearer the eighteenth-century design, figure 9, but that has the airy elegance of the period.

Early Windsors were made of several woods. The seat used a softwood that was easily carved to a saddled shape; the legs, stretchers, and front turnings under the arms were usually made of maple, as it turned to fine forms; and the back was of springy wood, such as ash or hickory, to take the pressure created by use. The whole was then united by paint, often black or green. The Brown University chair is appropriately painted, although it can be purchased in "natural birch" or "old pine"! But the chair is picked out in gold, a decorative idea employed *after* 1800 and therefore inappropriate on a chair that seeks to reflect the 1760's. If gold is used, it should probably be as in figure 9: on the legs it emphasizes the bigger rings, not the thin ones; and on the front arm supports it enriches the ring and reel turnings under the baluster turnings, not the thin rings; but although figure 9 is an eighteenth-century chair, the decoration is early-nineteenth-century! In some ways, the University chair is closer to figure 10, which also has a comb above the arm rail, but fortunately it uses fewer spokes than the Brown chair and pushes the crest up into the air with proper eighteenth-century open elegance; its crest rail is shaped to flowing movement whereas the top rail of the University chair is rather like a tired sausage. Interestingly, the University chair is, in its compact heaviness, more like figure 11, which is stamped T. SIMPSON BOSTON (figure 11a). (This would be unsuitable for any eighteenth-century American university, however, for it is not Boston, Massachusetts, but Boston, Lincolnshire, England, and early nineteenth century!)

What Brown University has provided is a chair that would never have been designed anywhere in America in the eighteenth century. We need not belabor the point further, but it must be recognized that this misuse of early ideas is no exception, and that Brown University is *not* at fault, for we are engulfed by similar clumsy ideas, by "neo-Howard Johnson's" taste; it is what the public has come to expect of "Americana." Perhaps in the dim future such objects will be looked back on as we now look back and prize the colonial revival of 1900, but what will be seen is the mid-twentieth century.

This bad taste, the perverting of an original concept which has great merit, is encouraged by the worse than inadequate ways in which early objects are shown to the public, usually in "historic houses." Many of these buildings never were of much architectural interest, and usually they now lack what little they had. It seems that most are stuffed with things from neighboring attics which, one has to conclude, always specialized in late-nineteenth-century bootees. When there is any early furniture, it is generally refinished to the point of non-interest.

A typical example of a "better" historic house open to the public is one at Wethersfield, Connecticut. Before its "restoration" it had nice but not spectacular architectural detailing, but what made it of more than general interest was the fact that it still contained some of the original

10. *Arm chair. Probably New England. 1750–1800. Courtesy, The Henry Ford Museum, Dearborn, Michigan.*

11. *Arm chair. For place of origin and date, see text. Photography, Courtesy, Victoria and Albert Museum.*

11a. *Detail of figure 11.*

furnishings. When it was "restored," however, both the house and the furnishings were "colonialized." For example, the original wide-board floors were sanded flat and varnished to a glossy newness when they should have been left beat-up and painted. The furniture was sent out to be cleaned of its original paint and surface: Queen Anne tables that had original red paint are now shiny maple-esque. This is a tragedy, for although the house was not of spectacular interest it was a good one. Had it been properly restored, using the original untouched (untouched means left alone and unrestored; old pieces have of course been touched by age) furnishings supplemented by untouched objects chosen and placed as suggested in early inventories, prints, and paintings; had it been preserved rather than reincarnated to suit the modern rich, it would have been worth visiting. Now it reflects only the taste of the sort of people who exclaim: "Oh, look at those wide-board floors," while ignoring anything rare or even slightly unusual.

In fact, wide boards do not signify rarity or greatness. They are available today, for a price, and if installed in this house and sanded and varnished to a glossy yellow they would look just like the present surface of the original eighteenth-century boards. But ruined or not, wide boards should not be raised to a status they never had— being then simply the cheapest way to cover a floor. The more expensive, narrowest boards are usually found on the first floor, slightly wider ones on the second floor, and the widest in the attic. We often prize what is rare now rather than what was rare or indicative of quality in the past. We are caught up in catch phrases and cute stories perpetuated by inadequately trained tour guides. Most early houses should be lived in by people who enjoy them for what they are, nice places to live, rather than having them opened to the public by people who pretend they are what they never were.

Part of our problem in fully perceiving anything today is the conscious misuse of words and objects by advertisers to numb—to prevent true perception of anything important. We are surrounded by the intentional misapplication of terms and a slurring of real meanings, so that words that once sparked a consciousness of recognition of important features, qualities, and values can be unconsciously attached to quite different, often shoddy things. They slip past without our noticing because we only attend to the catch word. In selling houses it is a "colonial," a "Cape," a "Queen Anne." For "colonial" decoration, the eagle is the preferred symbol—I have seen a gold plastic one in the center of a toilet seat—but a rifle, a wagon wheel, or even a horse will do. "Colonial" furniture includes anything with an eagle or lathe-turned elements; usually it must be shiny maple or birch, though it may be black and picked out in gold; where possible it has rockers; it should be decked out in some small-patterned textile, which is usually draped and pleated.

As words lose their meaning so do the ideas they describe. We have to fight to recognize what is being discussed, what is really being said. Even as I write I see on one of those plastic volumes for holding photographs the words "Virgin vinyl." Now virgin forest is one thing, and virgin wool may perhaps make sense to someone, but virgin vinyl . . .

MISGUIDED MOTIVES

It is intriguing and helpful to real perception to see where we get our strange, often very wrong, ideas about early furniture. Part of the problem is inadequate books, which confuse our values and blur our perceptions. I recently read such a book because it looked as though it was going to be quite terrible—it was. I find this to be a useful exercise, for such books make you say, "Oh, no," many times, and each shock shows you what

should have been said; it makes you aware of things you never knew you believed or felt strongly. Every time I said, "Oh, no," I wrote why I had said it on an index card, sometimes several, and thus began this manuscript. The book stressed the economic value of the pursuit of antiques, that one should choose what will increase in value. Seeking an object because it will increase in value is not and cannot be my approach. I want to be surrounded and confronted by great beauty—beauty of form, color, and pattern. (Incidentally, I have found that greatness of beauty does pay financially.)

Some years ago, I was told by a collector that he thought buying second-rate, B-quality items was a much surer investment, "For when the Depression comes there will be people with enough money to buy B-quality but no one to buy the first-rate." But during the Great Depression, this did not prove to be the case. People who had money saw it as a time to buy greatness cheaply, to select the best from the quantity that became available; and that is what is happening again. Great pieces are selling at seemingly fantastic prices, while the lesser are not finding as active a market. Buying first-rate objects, overpaying if necessary, is the most successful way to make money if that is what you want to do. This is as true for those who pay $6.00 for a chair as for those who pay $6,000.

There remains the question, Why do people collect? It is ridiculous to start purchasing without some idea of what you are looking for and why you want to buy it. Coming to understand the *why* will help you to focus on the *what*.

Most of us start with a vague and scattered notion of the kinds of things we want, but little idea of why we want them. As we progress, we refine our ideas because of a new understanding, and our likes and dislikes may shift, perhaps drastically, to a different taste, a different time of manufacture, a different kind of object; we may go from early slat backs to iron ice-cream-parlor chairs. Some change and refinement is inevitable. But looking, reading, and thinking before buying can prevent disposing of many objects after you find what you are seriously interested in.

At one extreme, the phenomenon of collecting develops from mania: licensed acquisitiveness, greed, and nostalgia (although the latter is put forward as one of the main reasons for an interest in early American objects, I think it is overplayed). At the other extreme, collectors purchase in order to create an environment that reflects their own tastes and personalities; milieus in which they can relax, where their eyes can at times play with delight and at times sink into quietness. The objects may also make the collector feel clever for managing fine investments and owning "unique" pieces.

But far more important is the setting in which a person lives, for objects condition as well as reflect their owner's mental state. No environment is unaggressive; it is constantly acting upon those who inhabit it. As early childhood experiences act on us for the rest of our life, the environment, the close surroundings, the rooms a person lives in, have an effect upon how he acts, what he is.

The first time I felt the impact of a consciously created environment was at the age of six, when my mother, brother, and I took a train from near Philadelphia to see New York. We went to the top of the Empire State Building of course and did all the other obvious things, but what I remember is our visit to Radio City Music Hall, that Art Deco wonder that is fortunately still just the same. There we joined a guided tour, and when we went into the lower lobby the guide said, "Since a movie will be going on most of the time upstairs, the designer realized that this huge lobby must be kept quiet. And how do you keep people quiet in a large space? The

designer decided to make it dark. Black glass on the supporting columns, and subdued colors for the rugs, upholstery, and walls." I have never forgotten that a man can affect the behavior, actions, and thinking of other men by giving them a particular setting.

Using early objects removes us from the plastic age where things tend to be immediate and hard, giving us a chance at softer lines and subtler colors. It is seldom recognized that these early pieces were once sharp-edged and aggressive, their colors not subdued; we perceive them now as quiet and soft for they have mellowed: shrinkage, air, light, and wear have made them that way.

Today, when painting a room or a piece of furniture in a "colonial" color, many people choose a paint that attempts to give it an instant, "early" mellow look. Usually such colors are subdued by the addition of white, which instead of making them interesting turns them into a milky mess. Genuine early paint is pleasing because it *started* beautiful and different areas of a piece or a room have faded to different shades, depending on how much light each received. (The famous orange-red room in the Villa dei Misteri at Pompeii has one window and the orange-red on the window wall is now much more intense than on the opposite wall.) The modern milky paints which I lump under the term "williamsburg blue" are not only terrible because of their nasty opaqueness, but they "mellow" all areas similarly. It is better to paint with a color that is like it was when first applied in the eighteenth or nineteenth century; it will not only be a better color, but with surprising quickness it will take on character. Even before it does, a *good* color will vary greatly according to whether it is in light or shadow. Alternatively, you could paint with a slightly lighter version of an original color and wash it darker where it should be darker. I have painted a room with a red-brown oil-base paint and washed areas darker with a very thin coat of black-brown water-base paint. The most successful new "old blue" room I have seen was in a private house in the Midwest; the owners had imported from New England excellent paint fakers, whose work is better known on old, and partly old, furniture.

Early, untouched objects make us feel we are coming into contact with something real, whether they are used in an early setting or one made of "glass and steel." If this is called nostalgia, all right; yet I believe it is not so much a desire for a feeling of being in the past as for objects that seem personal, individual. We do not recognize that some of them were turned out by the thousands.

I think what really matters in collecting is that pieces make an environment into which we can step, in which we can live, and where we feel things are genuine. Then there is the excitement of a close relationship with the things that you have chosen, that you have sought out and worked for, so that you do not feel you have gone to a store and purchased an instant interior.

2

The
Art
of
Looking

In the really bad book that I read before preparing this manuscript, I came across the remark that if you wish to collect profitably you must become an expert, and that it is not as difficult to become one as you may think; furthermore, it claimed, this would become apparent as you read. That is not true, and I find such a statement cruelly misleading. No one book can show an easy way to knowledge. The phrase I have heard most often from people who have spent their lives trying to understand American furniture is, "The more you know, the less you know." As I strive to perceive and understand, I realize that this is indeed true.

Recently, after spending two months in England studying the relationship between English and American furniture designs during the seventeenth and eighteenth centuries, I realized that many of my ideas about the Americanness of American objects were inadequate; although they had been formed during a year in England a decade earlier, there was a gigantic area of knowledge about which I knew very little. To say that you are going to become an instant expert means either that you have chosen a very small field, or a small facet of a larger one, or that your idea of knowledge is extremely limited. Certainly, there are forms or types of early objects about which there is not very much to know and if you confine yourself to them you will not have to do much work; but for anything more complex you need trained perception and vast "book knowledge."

TRAIN YOURSELF TO BE PERCEPTIVE

The first step in learning to perceive is to empty your mind of whatever you have been conditioned to think about the object you are approaching. During one of my first days as a serious student of early furniture I entered a room where there was, in pieces, a Shaker table with a tremendous one-board top, probably 15 to 18 feet long, and 3½ feet wide. I exclaimed, "What a magnificent table!" My teacher said, "It's a magnificent board." It *was* a wonderful board, but when placed on the pedestals that were its support it was not a particularly great table design. The *boardness* of the board had impressed me the way wide-board floors can impress the potential buyer of a mediocre house; and words like "Shaker" act on us like the bell on Pavlov's dogs. I had come to the table with the idea that anything that was Shaker was terrific, and anything with so large a board was wonderful; I did not *look* at the table as a table design.

Catchwords can keep us from seeing what is there. The myth persists that anything Shaker is great, and that anything simple is Shaker. It is impressive that workers in Shaker communities sought to make things not as personal accomplishments but as God's expression through them; yet it does not necessarily follow that all their objects were endowed with quality. Such an attitude might endow them with spirituality, but it does not necessarily give a maker with a poor sense of design the ability to achieve anything fine.

It is extremely difficult to approach an object freshly and without prejudice. Recently I gave a course in Providence, Rhode Island. Whenever an elaborately decorated piece of Philadelphia Chippendale furniture came on the screen, I heard mumbles of disapproval. The audience wanted the starker, more direct, less fussy New England taste, and automatically rejected any other interpretation of the style. Finally, when a slide of a superb, elaborate Philadelphia Chippendale highboy caused an unusual amount of disturbance, I whipped around from the great screen with its 20-foot image of one of the best designs ever made anywhere and shouted, "Stop being so damn provincial! *Look* at the object, at what the man *put* there—try to see what is *behind* and *in* that object. What is the nature of the design? What does it do to you? Then, if you don't like it after you have perceived it, fine —but just because a piece is different from what

you now find comfortable doesn't mean there's nothing there to be seen!"

The first exam I had on American furniture included a comparison of two New England dressing tables. Each had cabriole legs and four drawers. One was without decoration except for a patterned veneer; the other had a patterned veneer and inlaid star designs. I knew from studying the literature that these inlaid enrichments were rare and thus made the piece "very desirable" in the collectors/dealers market. Therefore, I chose as the better that with the star inlay. My teacher said simply, "Which one would you choose for yourself?" and I said, "Oh, the one without the decoration." When he asked why, I answered, "It's beautiful—each line is finely drawn and the response between curve and curve, and between curves and straights, is great; the other isn't as well designed." He said, "Well then, choose that one, too, for a museum."

One experience I remember as strongly as any was showing a Danish wax-dyed silk scarf in muted greens, yellows, rusts, and browns to someone who was studying a series of objects. Taking the scarf, she sat still for some minutes while I thought, "Oh, deep appreciation, understanding, perception!" In fact, this person had decided for the first time to look solely at color; to try to understand why colors themselves might be interesting. Previously, she had looked only in terms of black and white. Her main concern had been literature and the architecture of Cistercian abbeys, which can be perceived in black and white. This moment, this concentration, was the beginning of her awareness of a world that had hitherto been closed to her.

Beginning to look means bringing oneself to demand perception when you know there is something to be perceived. It is difficult to do this in a brand-new area, and even more difficult to force yourself to do it when you do not know, or are not sure, if there is anything there to be perceived. It is better to start therefore with objects that have been perceived and judged as good by others. They may have been wrong about a piece's relative greatness, but there is at least some surety that the pieces are worth your attention. To be assured of this, use books written by those long in the field and where possible by those who work with the objects professionally. The gifted amateur can be as scholarly and perceptive as the professional—often more so—but you can only judge others' competence when *you* know something. Whenever possible, bypass books, at least in the beginning, and go to real objects in museums.

What you should seek is that stage of perception where you begin to lose yourself in the object, where the world around it and you has less reality than your experience of the piece, when you and it advance toward each other and its "being" becomes available to you. There are tricks that one can use to get oneself closer to this state. It is possible to sit in front of an object and look at it until you are absolutely and utterly bored; you wish for lunch, a drink, any kind of relief, because you see nothing at all, or nothing interesting, or nothing new. It is possible to take out your watch then and say, "I will sit and look for ten more minutes," then, "I will sit and look for five more minutes," and then to keep on forcing yourself with five-minute intervals until something begins to happen (for some, shorter or longer forced intervals are better). If there is any quality there and you have opened yourself to it, it will appear. You will begin to see responses between parts; begin to see proportions; begin to see why the object has been selected by someone as a major work of art.

It is, of course, absolutely true that most objects do not merit this kind of concentration because there is little or nothing to be perceived; that is why you should start with the things con-

sidered great. If quality is there and you are open to it, it is possible to relax into it, but you should relax while forcing every sense to be actively, aggressively perceptive. I am forever seeing people going through a gallery bending forward and reading the labels, snapping their heads back to look at the objects for a shorter time than it took to read the labels, and saying, "Hmm," or, "I don't understand," or, "Why is that so great?" Then they move on to the next label, where they spend more time than with its object. Perhaps museums should show objects without labels, leaving the viewer on his own to relate to what is there, and provide information in a book by the exit door.

Years ago when talking with a curator of furniture at a major London museum I said, "Many of the labels are wrong," and he said, "But they were put there by my predecessor." I replied, "But they are *wrong*," and he said, "Those who know will know." And I said, "But this is a public institution, supported by public funds!" To which he said, "My dear boy, you care too much." It took me ten years to realize what he meant. We are all on our own. Yes, labels should be correct, but for many—those who are only label readers—it does not matter a great deal, and those who *look* at objects will soon know enough to realize when labels are wrong. Of course this leaves out those who expect to both look and read, but I think what he was saying is that it is the object itself that matters. Also, in the end, you have to rely on your *own* judgment.

None of us can be open to all things at all times. In shops I tend to skip the glass, pewter, china, and often the paintings, focusing on the furniture or the wooden objects. Because these matter to me, and because I constantly work with them, I can more easily approach them and more quickly reject those which are inadequate. My eye can skip those things which are lesser, and light on those which *might* please; but by doing this I also eliminate the possibility of seeing great things in areas with which I am not as familiar.

Another way to learn is to decide, without considering the prices, which item you would choose from a shop window or a stall at an antique show—not with the intention of purchasing it, but so that again and again you will face perception. This can be done while alone or with friends, and with modern and early pieces. I find it automatic as I await a bus or stagger through yet another antique show or shop. A variation, and one used by a Harvard history of art class, is to try to find the best piece priced under $50. The student who proposes the best buy is given his piece by Harvard.

Tuning your eye, opening yourself to design—whether early or modern—entails a constant renewal. Meyric Rogers, one of the great museum men, when he was about to look in antique shops in New York for possible purchases, would first walk through the American Wing of the Metropolitan Museum of Art, spending as much time there as possible. This was to get his eye in tune to quality so that when he arrived in a store he wouldn't say, "Oh, isn't that nice," about an object when it was not, but only seemed so because it was the best available or because a similar form had not been on the market for years. Like the amateur, those who are responsible for purchasing great objects, at great expense, for the very best museums have to keep their eye constantly in training, for maintaining a high degree of perception is a continuous process, as with a musician's or a sportsman's skill.

The problem with achieving a high degree of perception is that you may very quickly become dissatisfied with everything that surrounds you. It may make you intolerant and demanding. But

it will also give you the pleasure of honoring the good that you see. It gives you a chance to make nice things a part of your day-in and day-out life. You become more careful with them, but not because they are expensive—objects worth honoring are often less expensive than those given or purchased to make an impression. Once they are honored as fine, you will be more worried about their breakage than you were about the merely expensive, such as "impressive" wedding presents. When you pick up a chipped, beautiful pitcher you might take more care than you would with a lesser design from Steuben. But taking precautions may be hazardous for an object. After pointing out to some friends that the sherry glasses they were casually putting in their dishwasher were nice early-nineteenth-century ones, they decided, with my encouragement, that in future they would wash them by hand. The first time they did they broke the best one.

EVERYDAY OBJECTS

Figures 12 to 17 are the kinds of objects that we confront on a day-to-day basis. The ability to perceive them is the same ability needed to perceive all objects. True, they are not very rare, they are not seen only in antique shops, important private collections, museums, and historic houses; but perception of them and respect for superior designs can be practiced anywhere, at any time. It amazes me how people can acquire objects for daily use, things which they are going to handle and see constantly, without really thinking seriously about their design. Objects such as those in figures 12 to 15 are with us all the time. We handle them, we wash them, we store them, we hang them, they constantly bombard our eyes, and yet we often pay little conscious attention to them beyond their usefulness. Or, on the other hand, we buy them for their

12. Spoons, spatulas, and forks. Twentieth century.
Top row and H, J, and K, Courtesy, Chester
and Judy Michalik; others privately owned.

decorative quality, to hang on the wall, with little thought of whether they are also really useful, whether they are pleasing or miserably uncomfortable to use. Daily objects such as these should be useful, beautiful, and tactilely satisfying—a great design will be.

The three objects in the upper row of figure 12 are disasters as useful objects. The one on the left has a fish shape that makes the handle uncomfortable to hold, and it is coated with a red lacquer decorated with a black design; both come off in bits if the spoon is used in a salad or sauce. The large fork in the center cannot be used in a bowl with a rounded surface since it is wide and the teeth are all the same length; the center ones cannot touch a curved surface. Also, the handle does not allow for comfort or ease of grasp. The small fork on the right has two members that curve backward and jab the fingers of the users as they seek a pickle or smoked oyster.

The two wooden spatulas, A and B, in the bottom row have angled top edges; the one with the long handle twists in the hand as you use it because it is round, and when approaching a pan you must check each time to see if the flat or the narrow side is up; the hole in the center is hard to clean rather than useful. Spatula A has a shape beautiful to both eye and hand, although the top is correctly angled for only right-handed people; B, having a round handle, can be used by either. Plastic is often thought of as being more "practical" than wood. The plastic spoon, E, was white; it has discolored to an unpleasant yellow, whereas the wooden spoons, F to L, have aged to a beautiful color. It might be argued that wooden spoons do not do well in dishwashers, but neither do many plastic ones unless you want them to twist, discolor, and go matte. The ridges on the handle of E might be thought of as functional and decorative but they are not tactilely interesting, and dried materials such as flour and eggs have to be scraped from them. Round handles on spoons, in contrast to that on spatula B, are not as much of a problem. In using spoons one is more conscious of the bowl as it flows out of the handle; it seems part of what

you are handling. The two short spoons, G and H, have different handles: H is ovoid in cross-section and its base is bevelled from left to right. This is a particularly comfortable spoon for a right-handed person because the bevel fits into the palm as you stir. None of these objects is particularly old; most were bought new within the last twenty years, and the others were purchased for under fifty cents in junk shops. Thus, it is still possible to buy beauty and usefulness combined.

Figure 13 shows seven metal spatulas that illustrate the same kinds of choices confronting anyone setting up a household. Each has problems and advantages. First, let us consider how the surfaces condition their use. Spatulas B and D have their blades coated with a bright blue "non-sticking" surface, which is supposed to be an advantage. Instead, it makes the blades so thick that it is difficult to get them under a fried egg without breaking the yolk; and they cannot be used in a pan that is not similarly coated for

13. Spatulas.
Twentieth century.
Privately owned.

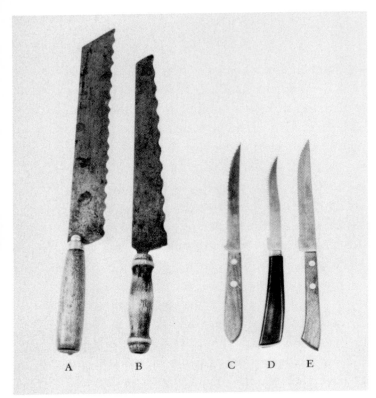

14. Knives. Twentieth century. Privately owned.

their round edges will not scrape loose anything that is stuck; the spoon from this set lost part of its bright blue covering in a dishwasher. Spatulas A, C, and G have regular steel blades which must be wiped dry after washing to prevent rusting, and C, F, and G have wooden handles that should not be soaked in water. E, with a plastic handle and a stainless steel blade, is "waterproof" and is therefore the most "practical," although it too would suffer in a dishwasher—the heat and strong soap would soon turn the plastic handle matte and probably eventually warp it. All present problems, so why not choose something that is beautiful and practical? The handles of B and D are not nicely shaped, although they pretend to be: the slight curve in at the base does not help the fingers grasp them, and while the back surface is rounded, they have an almost flat front surface for the placement of the "cute" decoration—perhaps their worst feature. I find I despise any object that carries such a decoration, for it is with you forever; it is aggressively present until you throw the thing out. My own

feeling is that the basic form should be beautiful and left undecorated. I do not like permanent things to be too bright, or strongly patterned. I think they should be quiet, and decorative accents should be made with disposable things: paint colors that can be changed, dishtowels and pot-holders that will eventually wear out. The aggressive features of a room should be easily and inexpensively changed.

In contrast to B and D, the handle of A is beautifully shaped aluminum, the under side comes around and wraps over the front face; it is attractive with its repeat of elongated outer and inner shapes, and it is nice to hold. The handle of C works well to the touch, and its roundness is not a problem as it was on B of figure 12, for the flat, spatula part is bigger and a sense of balance tells you whether a flat face or an edge is uppermost. Figures E, F, and G all have a useful downward angle between handle and spatula blade, making it possible for the blade to be flat on the bottom of a raised-edge pan. The blade of C is so flexible that it can achieve the same thing. Its slanted edge does cause some difficulty, for you have to be aware of which way it angles under certain circumstances. Each of these seven spatulas has its limitations and advantages; all have been found practical and useful except B and D, which recently were thrown out.

In figure 14 the two bread knives, A and B, are quite different. At first the handle of B looks as though it might feel better to the touch, but in fact one's fingers are never comfortable as they never know which side of the base ring to clutch. On A, this problem does not exist, and its slightly longer handle is more comfortable for most hands. The tapering of the blade of B does not help in cutting, and is thus no better than the parallel-sided blade of A. Of the small knives, E is miserable to hold, for the point of the handle's bevelled end jabs into the palm of both

15. *Pans. Mid-twentieth century. Privately owned.*

left- and right-handed users. Since it fits the palm beautifully, D is the most comfortable, and the handle flows nicely from the blade. C is perfectly satisfactory to use, and I personally prefer its shape. I like the similarly shaped sides on the handle playing against the asymmetrical design of the blade.

The two pans in figure 15 were made by the same company but were purchased thirteen years apart. The one on the left, which was purchased first, has a directness of design which I prefer. It has a thicker top rim, a deeper use of copper on the base, which gives a bigger horizontal base line, and a handle of simple, direct construction. The handle uses two pieces of metal that are bent at an angle and joined to the pan. These then pass up through the plastic part, which is made of two faces held in place by two visible bolts. The straight edges of the metal shafts have been maintained even where each joins the face of the pan. This makes for large visual and structural joining surfaces. There is a nice play of flat angle against round surface that seems immediate and simple; construction and design are one. This unity is furthered by being able to see the bolts that secure the plastic. On the pan at the right, the plastic handle is molded as one piece that encloses a metal shaft. The shaft is then wrapped by another piece of metal that is riveted to it; the end of this outer casing was rounded and then bent to right and left flanges that are fixed to the pan. One would think that round members would look better on a round pan, but they seem mincy and are badly shaped. They lack the strong visual statement found on the other pan. A further change that lessens the design is that the handle of the pan at the right joins the pan nearer the top edge; the lower placement on the left pan is better balanced both for eye and hand unless the pan is completely full; then the higher placement is better. The shape of the black plastic has also been redesigned for the worse; in the later version it has grown pudgy.

16. Volkswagen. 1955. Courtesy, Volkswagen of America, Inc.

The Volkswagens, figures 16 and 17, show a dramatic shift in design between 1955 and 1974. The demand for a larger engine, and the new safety regulations, have severely affected the visual impact of the later car. In figure 16, there is a finely integrated play of ovals: a long sweeping oval comes down from the top around the lower edge of the back lid, where it is formed almost to a point, and then curves back up the other side. About 4 inches in, there is another oval made by a crease which gives a repeating inner oval and also allows the outer edge to be raised in a dome that adds strength. These two lines diverge as they descend, spreading out their movement. Against these major ovals play the oval movements of the rear fenders. Above the back lid is a nearly oval window which allows you visually to pierce the object; below that is a strong fringe of air vent openings that again allows the eye to penetrate further into the metal, into the object itself. Since these are dark they form a row of mysterious, strong vertical shapes which arch to play against the oval of the back lid. In the center of the lid is a raised section that flares as it flows down. Just before it reaches the license plate light, the lines curve sharply out to play against the main outer ovals. Within this raised part is the small partial oval light whose movement is repeated on the fenders as the shape

17. *Volkswagen. 1974. Courtesy, Volkswagen of America, Inc.*

of the rear lights. All this movement and play of shapes is tied together by a shiny rear bumper whose rising pipes repeat the shape of the top of the window. This car shows a strong integration and echoing of related shapes. It is a totally unified concept.

On figure 17, a larger motor has meant more air vents, which have, unfortunately, been placed as a series of staccatoed horizontals below the original upper fringe of air vents. The oval of the rear lid has been flattened off at its base so that the lid can be brought up past the bumper, which has been raised to the new legal height. This raising of the bumper means that you can see below it to a part of the car that does not seem to relate to the upper part. The need for large rear lights and window has given us great aggressive areas that do not integrate into the design: the rear window is pushing against the inner oval of the top and the lights sit as great eyes. Everything is congested, large, and strangely unrelated in scale. The horizontal light over the license plate does echo the horizontal bumper; little else responds to any other part. Outside influences have forced changes in the design. Such influences are not unusual, but if you are going to change major parts of something that was once carefully organized, you usually have to scrap the whole concept and begin again from the beginning.

3

Knowledge

It is true to say that when an eye is properly trained, honed, and kept fit, great discoveries can be made. One can fall in love with a piece while having no knowledge about it, no idea when, where, why, or for what it was made, but a *real* understanding must include these factors. Understanding a piece involves a dual approach: perceiving it, what Martin Buber has called in another context an "I-thou" relationship, and knowing about it. It is not necessary that one of these precedes the other, although both will be part of complete enjoyment; and in buying, both trained eyes and knowledge must be present. Knowledge tells you that similar pieces were made at different times, revival following revival; a trained eye will help distinguish between them. Knowledge tells you that highboy tops are often sold as chests of drawers; a trained eye will tell you that it *looks* like a highboy top. Also, a good eye will stop knowledge from persuading you to buy something genuine whose only value is rarity.

Usually I experience three stages when I approach an object. The first is to react emotionally to its aesthetic impact. "It's marvelous," "It's awful," "How strange," "How fascinating," or "Good heavens" (which is itself ambiguous—it simply means I am taken aback and do not know which way to jump). Then second, if I have any serious interest in it, and that need not mean a desire to acquire it, I have to turn off my emotions and approach it as an abstract problem: Is the piece genuine and where does it fit into the history of furniture? To know its place in history is to know what went before, what was made at the same time, and what came after. Also, it is understanding how the object fitted into the original setting, how it was used and displayed.

The investigation as to genuineness can be a long process of searching to understand each and every unusual feature. For example, why are there nail holes when there is no board into which those nails could have gone? Does this mean that these are old boards made into a new form and the holes are from a previous use? Is an original part missing from an otherwise genuine piece, or has a board that was added later been removed recently?

A multitude of questions must be asked as one investigates each possibility. It is necessary to be a Sherlock Holmes of furniture. What kinds of nails and screws are present? Are they all of the same date? Does this agree with the date the style of the piece suggests? Are there early or late saw marks? (Circular saw marks would mean that the board was cut after the eighteenth century.) Does the interior have real age color or is it stained to look old? Are the interior boards of the drawers all the same color, showing that they have aged together? Have other parts been made to look old? Is the wear consistent with the real use of that kind of piece? Was it painted, and if so what was the original color; is it still there (perhaps just in the cracks)? As you look, questions by the dozens may be raised by unusual features and peculiarities. The famous early-twentieth-century collectors did this sort of investigation on each piece, but many now tend to want dealers to do it for them!

If a piece withstands such a rigorous investigation, then the third stage, the return of the initial emotions which made you look at and react to it, combines with your knowing it to be genuine: eye *and* knowledge. You will now not only have a greater enjoyment of the piece but it will be an object that interests you longer.

Limited knowledge can be dangerous. The mistakes that I have made have been in grabbing or reaching out for objects that I "knew" to be rare: a slat-back chair with "Queen Anne" feet and a "Massachusetts" Chippendale chair with scroll feet. I rushed in to make a buy. I did not really like them, I did not find them beautiful, and had I consulted my aesthetic judgment I would not have wanted them. This is not just knowledge in retrospect for I was never overwhelmed by their beauty; rather, if they were what I was sure they were, then they were being offered at too low a price. The slat-back chair with Queen Anne feet was not under-priced, for it is a type standard in the north of England! The shape of the back of the Chippendale chair had suggested that it was a Massachusetts chair, and there is one Massachusetts chair with related scroll feet. The near uniqueness of the newly found chair added zest. Again, the problem was that I did not know that such backs and feet are found in England.

A little knowledge can often be a handicap, particularly if you ignore aesthetics in your excitement. If you only know enough to make you jump for an object you think you understand, and particularly if you have had good luck once and almost by accident made a killing, you are likely to take a chance. Recently a young collector bought for one-fourth of its value a nice Queen Anne, Massachusetts highboy. A month later he almost snapped up another that was an early-twentieth-century rebuilding of an eighteenth-century one. He could hardly wait to hand over the money he had borrowed that day to pay for it. He had studied the first highboy in detail as he was surprised to find it, especially at the price. But only a glimpse at the second had sent him running to the bank feeling that first-rate things were seeking him out. There are too many wrong pieces around that are not as presented to take chances without careful analysis of their aesthetics and genuineness.

Basic knowledge includes knowing where an object fits into the sequential development of a form. The illustrations in this chapter show the development of three basic forms of American furniture, although each has close English ancestors: the slat-back chair made from about 1690; the Windsor chair made from about 1740; and the six-board chest made from about 1680. All three forms continue to be made. Each grouping shows a sequential development of form and

18. Arm chair. Connecticut, Norwich area (letter from Benno Forman, September 1973). 1700–1735. Courtesy Knut Ek.

decoration and demonstrates how each piece is best first understood against what went before, what happened at the same time, and what came after. Knowing this, you will know whether it has the right kinds of features: whether some have been removed or added and whether it is early or late within its period or a revival. By understanding what all versions of a form looked like, you can better judge each expression.

SLAT BACKS

One of the earliest forms of chair used in America has been called a ladder back but is now more accurately called a slat back, referring to the members of the back as horizontal slats rather than suggesting that they are like rungs in a ladder. This form was first made on the continent; the idea went to England, and in the late seventeenth century, about 1680 to 1690, traveled from there to America. Its design principle is simple and basic—an assemblage of vertical and horizontal sticks. Four big corner posts are connected by horizontal pieces that form the back, arms, seat rails, and stretchers. The slats of the back are made of thin wood, enabling them to be bent to give the sitter some comfort. Often the members are kept from falling apart by small pegs placed through the back posts and the top slat; such pegs may also secure other joints such as lower slats and arms (figure 4). But what really holds it together is the rush seat. Without removing the seat it is impossible to get the chairs apart. From the earliest times cattails, an easily obtainable material, were used to make a woven seat (figure 18). Later, splint seats (figure 21) were also used. Splints are strips of thin wood peeled from logs. At first this form of chair seems very simple, almost rudimentary, in design, but that is not really true. They could have been made of unturned boards only smoothed enough to prevent chafing, and there is a Canadian tradition of such chairs. The makers of chairs like those included here not only turned most of the parts round on a lathe but also ornamented them.

In the history of furniture design, in the history of decorative arts in general, one finds that the maker will lift the object, the useful, functional thing, into an art object if he can. By art object I mean one enriched in design so that the beholder, the person coming toward it, would enjoy it visually as well as being able to use it. It was to be judged aesthetically as well as practically; it is therefore useful sculpture. A maker lifts an object from being merely utilitarian to the degree that he has artistic skills. Often what the maker can execute is conditioned by the amount the buyer is willing to spend, for he had to pay for the time given to each area of ornamentation.

Early slat backs, such as figure 18, display a directness of form whose parts have such a scale that you feel the woodness, almost the trees from which they were made. As in most great designs, the ornamentation echoes back and forth across the chair: on the front posts, under the arms, is a baluster shape which appears twice on each back post; the elaborately turned finials, with centrally accented egg shapes (originally there was an elaborate tip on top of these), terminate the back posts with the most decorative feature, punctuating the upper corners of the design. The tops of the front posts need to satisfy both visually and functionally, for the hand of the sitter would constantly be in contact with them. So they are flat. When you sit in the chair and put your hands on these hand holds, you get a proper sense of being in command of the space around you. Such chairs were reserved for the most important people, while others sat on stools or benches. The shape of the parts and the way they are combined make figure 18 dramatic, but this drama is rendered more forceful by the use of black paint.

Such pieces should always be painted, for this is the final act of the designer-maker, his means of unifying the design and intensifying the silhouette. These chairs are usually made of several woods and their various grains and colors must not be seen. When the paint is original or early it should not be touched. Even if there are layers on layers, they should all remain if they are making an interesting worn surface; the history of the object should be left intact for that is what makes it old. If, of course, it is painted with silver or gold "radiator paint" then you will want to remove that, but the next beautifully worn layer should be preserved.

This chair too provides an exception to the "Don't touch it" rule. Slat backs are bilateral designs; most of the decoration is pushed to the sides and builds to terminate in elaborate finials. These active sides are connected by simple-shaped horizontal pieces. In the late nineteenth or early twentieth century, somebody painted flowers on the slats, and they add a central accent which should not be there. Without touching the black paint, the posies should be removed; but this must be done by a trained painting restorer, for what has happened to figure 4 must not happen to figure 18, indeed, should not happen to *any* chair.

Figure 19 has a powerful design with deep, rich turnings. The hand-hold terminals of the front posts are, on this chair, the same size as the posts; the finials with their exciting change from wide rings to narrow areas are marvelous. But this chair has been diminished, for the final organizing statement of the maker, its paint, is gone. The intensification of the design is gone. The powerful silhouette is gone. It is now a lesser object than it once was.

Figure 20 is not as great an object as figure 19 was. It does not have deep ring turnings and the finials are smaller, but it has a terrific surface with an incredible orange-red paint. The lighter turnings of this New England chair determine

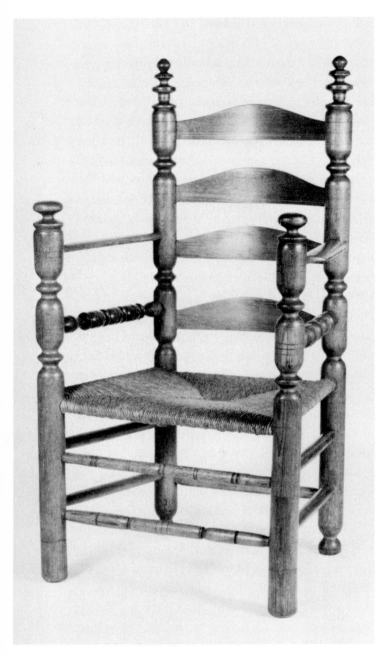

19. Arm chair. Southeast Massachusetts. 1690–1710. Courtesy, Museum of Fine Arts, Boston.

that it was made later than figure 19; probably it is early eighteenth century, and it looks it. All of its age is present: the top edge of the top slat looks as though a rat has chewed it away. The flat arms have slight saw marks along the edges; probably someone once used it as a sawhorse. In places the beautiful paint is worn away to the wood, and the surface of the wood itself has developed rich character: the soft grain has shrunk away, leaving the hard grain prominent, creating an exciting texture. Unfortunately, the hand holds, the terminals of the front posts, are gone. Do you restore them? No, because you do not know what shape they were. If one had survived you might consider restoring the other. But we do not know what they looked like and the present top surface of the front posts is superbly worn, beautiful to eye and hand. If I had to decide between figures 19 and 20, I would choose figure 19 as a statement of the highest level of achievement in the early slat backs. But to live with, I would choose figure 20. It has age and character—all its history.

The next stage in slat-back development is seen in figure 21. This chair has broad hand-hold terminals on the front posts, which have fantastic wear: the left one (figure 21a) has been whittled and played with until it has developed a personality that almost speaks. Such "mushrooms" came into being between 1690 and 1700. Is that then the date of this chair? No. There are later features and you must always date an object by its latest feature. An earlier feature can appear later for many reasons; it can be used forever once it has become part of the design vocabulary, but a late feature cannot be used before it was invented. Well, what are the features we have not seen before? We have not seen "sausage-turned" arms and front stretchers, and they *began* about 1710. The latest features, however, are the thinness of the posts, the delicacy of the finials, and the thinness of the ring turnings.

21. *Arm chair. New England; possibly New Hampshire. Late eighteenth century. Privately owned.*

20. *Arm chair. New England. 1700–1735. Seen also in figure 87. Privately owned.*

21a. *Detail of figure 21.*

22. Side chair. Rhode Island. Recently found in the attic of the Ananias Mowry House, North Smithfield; built about 1750. (Files of Slater Mill Historic Site.) 1750–1800. Privately owned.

The once-thundering ring accents are now diminished to thin horizontal lines. We must date this chair when such thinness became popular, in the last quarter of the eighteenth century, 1775–1800.

What happened from about 1800 to modern times is that the ring turning disappeared, and plain, undecorated posts were used (figures 3 and 23). Some chairs, such as figure 22, have a combination of plain and decorated posts, suggesting that they were made after ring turning began to disappear. This development may also be the result of an earlier aesthetic or economic simplification. Figure 23 is probably mid- to late-nineteenth-century; it could be as late as 1900. Thin, tapering back posts rise to skinny finials; skinny arms top the front posts; there are plain, almost dowel-like stretchers. Such a chair should not, however, be viewed as a degenerated eighteenth-century concept; it is an entirely new idea in design. Where figures 18, 19, and 20 were vigorous, active designs, this was made to suit a new, quieter aesthetic.

When there are rockers, there is always the question whether they are original; many early chairs had them added when rocking came into fashion in the beginning of the nineteenth century. We know that those of figure 23 are original for they have the same paint history as the rest of the chair; the entire chair has the same three layers of paint—an original red paint, then a later blue, and now gray. If the rockers had only blue and gray paint we would know that they had been added when the chair was painted blue. There are, however, two possible exceptions to using such evidence. The rockers could have been replaced, if they had worn or broken, and red paint was often used as an undercoat, making the second the original finish color. (Often pieces are taken back to their "original red" when this was their original undercoat.) It is possible, since early painters were as lazy as we, that they did not bother giving an undercoat to the rockers. By wear evidence you may be able to determine whether the red was an undercoat; if both the red and the blue have the same history of wear, then both are original. On figure 23 all three colors are on all members. The chair has a good all-over quality to its surface, except on the outer face of the left front post where some idiot, wanting to know what kind of wood it was, scraped away the paint to find out. Had it been maple, a wood which "refinishes beautifully," it would now look like figure 4. Fortunately, it was birch and the destruction went no further.

Figure 3 is the kind of chair still being made in various rural areas of America. The design may seem minimal, stripped to bare essentials, but it would have served the same purpose—if by purpose we mean simply use—if the posts had been left unturned. But it is lifted above function and asks to be judged aesthetically. Most of the parts are turned, the back slats are shaped with top arches to give visual lift, decorative finials terminate the back posts, and it was painted dark red. It is a simple, basic piece of art. The original thin coat of paint is properly worn on the front stretchers, the tops of the front posts, the upper fronts of the back posts, and the finials. The seat has been properly restored with splints. It is usually possible to ascertain which type of seat was originally used, if it is now missing, by studying the seat rungs, for the original material made deep imprints on the fresh wood: narrow, roundish dents mean rush; broad, flattish dents indicate splints.

Figure 24 was made in a Shaker community about 1820 to 1870. Such objects have been seen as a breakthrough in design, but despite what is generally believed the Shakers did not—as a result of their retirement from the world and their focus on spiritual things—create a radically new concept of design contrary to their surrounding world. They were not the first, as we too readily accept, to cut through all that "over-

23. Arm chair. Probably northern New England. Second half of the nineteenth century. Privately owned.

24. Rocking side chair. New York. Shaker Community of Watervliet. (Museum files.) 1820–1870. Courtesy, The Henry Francis du Pont Winterthur Museum.

elaborate Victorian enrichment" and get down to basic design. Prior to the Shakers' concentration upon furniture design, objects such as figure 3 were in existence. Simple, plain, direct, and therefore inexpensive design had long been common. The men who went to Shaker communities and formed their taste in furniture selected one from the various approaches already existing. Their main aesthetic act was to choose *this* particular taste rather than some other from the many available. It is interesting that, according to tradition, their founder, Mother Anne, kept with her a chair with ring turnings on its posts. And, it should be noticed that such chairs as figure 24 do not, in fact, strip away all decoration: the back posts terminate in "useless" finials, the slats are arched, the front legs taper to the rockers, and it employs a fancy-grained wood, tiger maple.

The chairs in figures 18 to 23 show a logical progression from one taste to another. It would be possible to see the change as only a simplification, perhaps a weakening, of ideas—the influences of laziness and modifications brought about by a changing economy and the emergence of the machine age. It might, however, be fairer to see these stages of the slat back as reflecting the changing taste in all forms of furniture. Figure 21 introduces a lightness in keeping with the new fashion for lighter, more airy objects introduced in urban centers after 1790 in shield-back and square-back chairs as part of the Early Classical Revival. Figures 23 and 24 reflect membership in their century's simple, cheap, vernacular furniture.

When presented like this, the history of the slat back seems a simple, logical sequence, and it is indeed lovely to have such a straightforward progression of change; when we find a slat-back chair, need we simply measure the size of the posts and their rings when they are present to know its date? Unfortunately, this will not do. There are always exceptions. There are always rural places that do not reflect new ideas, tending to resist what is "foreign"; also, in both rural and urban centers, there are always old customers who want something to "match" what they have. One famous example is that of Queen Marie Antoinette, who in 1780 ordered a *retardataire* "secretaire" from Jean-Henri Riesener, her favorite cabinetmaker, for use at Versailles. This employed the style of the 1760's.* Such instances cause problems in dating by features. Usually, however, a person working "out of style" will show it by introducing something from his own time. Another complicating factor is regional difference—the variation in design approach between one region and another. We are not surprised when pieces of Dutch, French, and English furniture use the prevailing style differently. The same types of differences are found between areas of America, which were often more geographically and sometimes culturally separate than some European cultures. The fact that most of the early East Coast settlers came from England makes their products similar, but before the first immigration, different areas of England were already interpreting basic styles differently. These differences were preserved and continued in America because immigrants tended to come with and settle with people from their former community.

The chairs in figures 18 to 23 were made in New England, while figure 25 was made in the New Jersey–Pennsylvania area and exhibits a different idea of what a slat back should be. It may at first seem like a nineteenth-century New England chair, but there are differences. The back posts taper to the finial and this appeared on only one New England chair, figure 23, which

* Trevor J. Fairbrother, in conversation, December 1974; described in F. J. B. Watson, *Wallace Collection Catalogues Furniture* (London: William Clowes and Sons Ltd, 1956), F 300, pp. 149–53 and plate 86, F 102, p. 71.

25. Side chair. Delaware River Valley. 1750–1810. Courtesy, Yale University Art Gallery; The Mabel Brady Garvan Collection.

was very late; the finial uses an acorn form that became standard in this middle states area; the slats are serpentine on both top and bottom edges; the bases of the back posts taper sharply to the floor; the front legs are turned below the seat to a ball and reel form that together makes a baluster shape; and these legs terminate in feet that are turned to a flattened ball with a reel turning above and a blunted point below. The front stretcher uses two baluster turnings either side of a central ring flanked by reel turnings. Similar front stretchers did appear about 1700 on New England bannister-back chairs but were not used on New England slat backs until much later; they are known on the early Pennsylvania-area slat backs, however. Figure 25 uses a trick seen often on chairs from its area: it is made of striped or tiger maple, coated with a thin, dark red-brown finish. The figure of the wood shows through the dark finish to give the impression of fashionable figured walnut or mahogany.

WINDSORS

The Windsor is another type of chair which has remained popular since it was first made. The earliest American Windsors date from the mid-eighteenth century, around 1740. As with any long-popular form, what it looked like at any given moment depended heavily on the prevailing taste in furniture. Although new attitudes toward design changed the shapes of its parts and altered its general "feel," it has continued to be made in the same way. Much of its popularity derives from its sound use of materials. Wood is very strong if you utilize its strength and do not cut into its long grain. Windsors take advantage of this. The top rails of chairs such as figure 26 are bent strips whose grain follows round the shape of the arch which encloses the spokes. If, instead of bending, a similar curved shape had been cut out from a wide board, it could have

broken in all the places where the grain was short.

What classifies a chair as a Windsor is that it has a wooden plank seat into which sticks are stuck. The parts do not need to be artistically designed; they could be branches torn from a tree and stuck into a plank and such a piece would still be classified as a Windsor. But, of course, pieces are lifted into art objects when their parts are made to be beautiful and their all-over appearance pleasing. The continuous arm, bow-back Windsor, figure 26, is one of the greatest achievements of this form. Each leg is a masterful design, moving down from the seat in a partial, then complete baluster form, and then into a thin, reel-shaped neck which goes out to a ring above the taper to the floor. Such dramatic changes from thick to thin parts are possible because maple is used. Not only does it have sufficient strength to allow the reel to make such a thin accent, but its close grain made possible the elegantly smooth, sharply turned edges at the top of the baluster and on the reel, without the pockmarks an open grain would cause. The counterpoint between similar parts of the chair is excellent. The shaping of the four legs is used under the front arms. Further, this echoing of design is made more exciting by the action and tension caused by the differing angles of thrust: the legs thrust up and in, the arms up and out. These thrusts result from the maker's desire for greater stability (achieved by broadening the stance of the chair below) and greater space for the sitter above. The turned arm supports carry the beginning of the top rail, which sweeps in, then up and around the rayed spokes of the back, containing them both functionally and aesthetically. This chair is one of the great American achievements, superbly combining aesthetics and construction. Indeed, it is one of the greatest American Windsor chairs, except for one thing: its lack of paint. You should not be able to see the varying grains—springy ash for the back, easily carved tulip poplar for the seat, and maple for the main turnings. The original maker would find the varying wood grains and color detrimental to his design. Today we have become used to all this woodiness, but it is distracting since we read the chair in three areas which paint would have made one. This chair has been diminished aesthetically, as a document, and monetarily by the fool who cleaned it.

Figure 27 is a lesser chair. At least it originally was so, for the movement of the turning, although good, is not as exciting, not as beautifully drawn. Its leg turnings do not swell way out and go way in, but it does have its paint— a beautiful surface of purply-red paint aged to great character. Not only is the paint worn away in places but the wood of the inner face of the front arm supports has also been worn away by countless sitters. It is like a used soap figure that has begun to melt away and soften in outline. If I had to choose between figures 26 and 27 it would be very difficult because the first was, and still is, a greater form, a greater concept by a greater artist; but figure 27 shows its age, it has an old surface. Figure 26 is very much like a copy. It is not as near to the original as an exact copy that included paint.

Figures 26 and 27 were made in the second half of the eighteenth century, 1750–1800, and are dynamic designs. They thrust into and play with the space around them. About 1790, the new Early Classical Revival swept America. A whole new concept of design took over. Tables developed tall, thin legs; objects stood quietly in space with air playing through them; they were leanly elegant, and Windsor chairs changed as did slat backs to relate to their new contemporaries. Figure 28 is typical of the new taste. The legs do not rake out as strongly, and their movement from floor to seat is gentle. The centers of the two swelling areas are accented with grooves

26. Arm chair. Probably New England. 1750–1800. Courtesy, Yale University Art Gallery; gift of C. Sanford Bull.

27. *Arm chair. Probably New England. 1750–1800. Privately owned.*

to make the legs look like bamboo. The seat too is quieter. No longer does it yank itself up in the center but gently and serenely moves through a horseshoe shape. This horizontal pattern is also used in the vertical for the shape of the back. The spokes are more parallel to each other and have a quieter relationship to the top rail. This new taste for quiet and elegant serenity was not confined to furniture but permeated everything: architecture, clothes, all that goes into making up a cultural moment.

In England, the legs and other turned parts of Windsor chairs were usually made of elm or beech, neither of which encouraged, as does maple, the turning to thick and thin parts with sharply turned edges, the hallmarks of quality for eighteenth-century American Windsors. Nor in England was there the grand raking of the legs that, with the appropriate raked arm supports, makes American Windsors so active. Figure 29 is an English Windsor of some merit. It is better than its compatriot, figure 11, whose late date makes it compatible with figure 28. Figure 29 has more movement in the back than many English Windsors, the form of the front arm supports is reversed end for end in the shaping of the legs, the legs are more raked. Nevertheless, it lacks the excitement of related American chairs such as figure 9.

Eighteenth-century excitement can also be found in American comb-back Windsors. The leg turnings of figure 30 would by themselves make this a major object and their design is stretched and echoed in the turned outer spokes of the back. As bow-back Windsors shifted from exciting active designs with baluster shapes, so did comb-back Windsors. Figure 31, with its strong swellings accented by grooves, shows the new taste of 1800 to 1830. After that, the swelling decreased until by the mid-nineteenth century the turning was almost straight, with only slight concave shaping between its grooves.

28. *Side chair. Possibly New England. 1800–1830.*
Courtesy, Yale University Art Gallery; The Mabel
Brady Garvan Collection.

29. *Arm chair. England. 1750–1800. Courtesy,*
Parker Knoll Ltd., High Wycombe, Bucks.

30. *Side chair. Probably New England. 1750–1800. Privately owned.*

31. *Side chair. Possibly New England. 1800–1830. Privately owned.*

32. *(right) Chest. New England. 1680–1700. Privately owned.*

Unfortunately, figure 31 does not have a glorious coat of paint; it has been cleaned but not skinned (that is, it has lost its paint but not the top surface of its wood). The careful removal of a nasty, heavy coat of recent paint revealed this light wood surface. The original coat of red-brown must have been very thin since there are only traces of it.

By learning which shapes were made when, it is possible, as with slat backs, to date Windsors, but, as always, one must be on the lookout for exceptions.

SIX-BOARD CHESTS

One of the first forms of furniture was the chest, and it served many purposes. You could sit on it, store or ship things in it, sleep in or on it, and use it as a table. The early box form of chair developed from it. In seventeenth-century New England, chests were the main storage units, for there were

few clothes cupboards; true, there were not many clothes, but what there were would be stored in a chest. Historically, there are two ways to make chests. The more elaborate were framed together: corner posts and horizontal rails connected by mortise and tenon joints, and the spaces filled with panels. But the more ancient form, the six-board chest, which had become less popular than the framed form during the seventeenth century, did at the end of that time regain its role. Since then it has, by using the simpler method of construction, remained common. It is formed of just six planks (figure 32): to a bottom board are nailed two end boards which continue down past it to form the feet: a central notch in the bottom of each end board creates front and rear feet; then the front and back boards are nailed into place, and finally the top is hinged onto the back board.

Figure 32 is an early New England chest, 1680 to 1700, made of thick and rugged planks

33. Chest over drawer.
Probably eastern
Massachusetts. Dated
1702. Courtesy, Museum
of Fine Arts, Boston.
Bequest of Charles
Hitchcock Tyler.

34. Chest over drawer.
New England. 1700–
1735. Central brasses
original, side brasses old
but not original; they
should be quatrefoil in
shape. Courtesy, Roger
Bacon.

held together by big-headed nails, which were of course hand-made. It could have been left plain and would have been perfectly useful, but it was, naturally, ornamented. This was done in a simple manner, with a molding plane, which is much like a regular wood plane except it has a shaped blade that can dig a decorative line. With a molding plane the maker easily dug a horizontal line (called a shadow molding) across the front about a quarter of the way down, producing a broad area below and a narrow one above; he also molded the lower front edge. These moldings and the resulting broad flat areas intensify the horizontal action of the front board, the front façade. To terminate this action, the front ends were ornamented with similar ease. With a chisel the maker repeatedly dug out little bits to make a vertical serrated line. He did the same across the end of the top board. How simple the means and how rich the effect. And then, of course, he painted it. It has a soft, darkish brick color, which in places has faded to a soft pink-red. After three hundred years of use the paint has worn from the top. Here is everything that makes an object old, and it is beautiful.

What happened next to the chest form was that the simple six-board object was raised in the air and a drawer placed below to produce a piece like figure 33. It has bottom, end, front, back, and top boards, but the ends are longer to pass and hold the drawer; the bottom board of the chest section is, of course, above the drawer. This obvious progression of ideas came from Europe to America about 1670 to 1680. Figure 33 is ornamented the same way as figure 32: a plane dug out horizontal lines across the front, but similar decoration goes up the end boards. The horizontal action across the front is stopped by much smaller vertical chip carving, which is wonderfully quick in its action, looking as if a mouse had rapidly eaten up the corner. Although this piece can be easily described in the same terms as figure 32, it *looks* very different.

Should it look so different? No, at least not as much as it does. The damage to this piece is its loss of original paint. That which should organize it has been thrown away, and the shadow moldings have since been painted red and black; like rubbed-in streaks of mascara they slash across the front between wide areas of grainy pine. Such pieces were meant to be painted an all-over color, as were the floors on which they stood; then features might be picked out in contrasting colors. The present state of discord would never have been tolerated. Despite its damaged condition, figure 33 is still an important object, for it is dated 1702. Since the date appears genuine (something that is not always the case since dated pieces are loved by collectors and their helpmates, the fakers), we know when it was made, and thus it becomes an important document in fixing the time of such moldings, chip carving, the use of a single drawer and wooden knobs. This is no longer an art object but it is an important document, a historic artifact, revealing part of what was done when. But what it really looked like when its maker finished it and its first owner possessed it, what they both wanted, we do not know.

The next development was to use all drawers, an idea that came from Europe just before 1700. On figure 34 you see the new, quieter horizontal areas created by using all drawers, and the half-round moldings which surround them. Also, for the first time there are brasses, beautiful shiny brasses. You can now buy pre-tarnished brasses that have been lacquered so that they always appear dirty, which is absolutely ridiculous. Brasses were meant to be shiny. They were the highlights, the sparkling accents, and, according to Benno Forman, they could be purchased, at least by the mid-eighteenth century, with a coat of varnish to protect their *shine*. This piece, as

35. *Chest over drawer. New England; possibly Rhode Island. 1820–1840. Courtesy, Mr. and Mrs. Bayard Ewing.*

seen originally by night, would have been illuminated only by a candle or a flickering lamp or fire; the painted wooden part would have receded into the shadows and the brasses would have twinkled and winked at you. Not only are these brasses the most prominent accents, but they also provide important visual organization. The lock, and therefore its escutcheon, had to be placed near the top edge of the drawer so that the bar of the lock could engage the rail above. The pulls were placed logically halfway down the drawer. Therefore each drawer area acquired from its three brasses an arching line.

Well, I've been fooling you. This is not really a chest of drawers, it is a chest over one drawer. The top two drawers are faked onto the front of a chest section that they disguise. Visually this *is* a chest of drawers, however. It was to *look* like a chest of drawers to meet the taste demands of the time. It had to look like a chest of drawers because that was the fashionable object. On entering a room you *saw* a chest of drawers; but while the purchaser wanted fashion he also wanted a piece that would serve established habits. This contrast between fashionable exterior and useful interior is one of the first instances of what will remain a tension between the two. The piece has a rich, soft blue color, which is a nineteenth-century paint over the original red; but this surface should never be touched, for it has developed a fine character and the blue has faded beautifully.

The next development was to place a chest of drawers on a chest of drawers, and we call it a chest-on-chest. Also, a chest of drawers was placed on a stand with long legs, and usually containing drawers, and we call it a highboy.

The sequence at its simplest, then, is a con-

36. Chest. New England. 1790–1820. John T. Kirk.

tinual development from the basic six-board chest to the sophisticated highboy. However, as in other forms, the development is not so clear that at each stage all direct precursors lose their aesthetic or functional merit and cease to be wanted or needed. In the rural areas older fashions tended to linger, but that is not the only reason for late examples of earlier forms. Even in the most developed houses in the most urban centers where highboys would occupy prominent positions there was still a use for a chest, whether it was only a simple, six-boarded one (figure 36) or one with a drawer such as figure 35.

Although similar in form, figure 35 hits any viewer as something very different from figures 33 and 34: there are no moldings, shadow or applied, and no enrichment except the patterned paint and large, turned wooden knobs. Is it the

same as the 1702 piece? Does this piece *say* 1702 to you? No, it is not the same, but a new statement. How do you date it? You could look at the nails and hinges and see that they are nineteenth-century, but you do not need to go inside this piece to see constructional details—you need only look at the exterior. The taste of this original paint, so different from the shadow moldings, says 1820 to 1840, as do the broad walnut knobs so unlike the tiny knobs on figure 33. At the time this was made, the taste in expensive pieces was for elaborately grained mahogany. To reflect that, this piece was first painted yellow and when that had dried the painter took red-brown paint on a piece of twisted paper or a sponge and made an elaborate "mahogany grain." On the drawer, around the knobs, the grain effect is quite real, but on the chest section above, freedom prevailed. The decoration just splashes and dances,

37. *Chest. Possibly New England, possibly Canada. Late nineteenth century. Courtesy, Joyce Harpin Charbonneau.*

plays and swirls like great worms moving back and forth across the surface. The sides are different; they are quieter, with shell-like patterns. This chest has an absolutely marvelous quality in its color and pattern.

Thank goodness that what happened to figure 38 did not happen to figure 35, for the former now has a brand-new maple surface. It has been so severely sanded that you cringe. One wishes it had been burned instead of being skinned to naked rawness. There is absolutely nothing left. It looks like a supermarket special. It is awful. It should be seen with its front pushed against the wall, for the only old part is the back, which was not touched and retains a fine, aged color. Figure 36 is now a strong powder blue. This is not its original color, for the blue covers the lock

escutcheon and some deeply worn areas, but it has probably been there from the mid-nineteenth century and has aged to great quality. The form of the nails and the oval shape of the escutcheon suggest that it was made about 1800. Its importance lies not in its earliness or rarity, for thousands of similar chests are known, but in its color and the condition of the surface, without which the piece would be just a box. Figure 37 is *totally* dependent on its paint, for it is basically a clumsy late-nineteenth-century form with awkward legs, lifted to fascination only by its superb dark brown painted grain.

Knowledge is not just knowing the sequential development of forms, it is also knowing exceptions and how at each stage the pieces were finished. It is having a firm grasp of what a piece from any given period *should* look like. When you know the development *and* its exceptions then you can see an object in terms of its peers, can realize what went before, what led up to it, helped create it, and can see what it helped produce. To this you need to add your own evaluation of what has happened to it: its present state, any repairs or changes, and its surface. Does it show its history? Has it developed an interesting character? Next, to this factual knowledge you must add your perception of form, line, and balance. Only then can you begin to judge whether an object is a good piece of American furniture, perhaps a great piece of American furniture, or, like so much, simply old.

38. Chest over drawers. New England. 1770–1810. Courtesy, Knut Ek.

4

What
Is It?

Knowledge of a tradition, of what a piece should be like, understanding it in terms of its contemporaries, not only helps you date long-continuing forms such as slat backs and Windsors, it also makes it possible in many cases to see where a piece has been restored incorrectly or where a faker working outside the time of the initial idea has added something that is foreign, something that should not be there. Furthermore, it can make you understand and appreciate an object that has been altered during its life in a way that makes it now extremely interesting and worth collecting. Many pieces have been changed since their initial creation, not with the intention of faking them to look more expensive for modern audiences, but by an owner who altered an old form to meet a new taste or need, or because repair was necessary after severe damage. Such legitimate "folk" changes or repairs were usually done in the contemporary taste or style and these pieces can be visually exciting in having a combination of early and late features. A piece may be an interesting

example of a culture's preservation of objects from an earlier time and as such a way of perceiving a moment in America's past.

Knowing what should be there in front of your eyes has to include an understanding of strangeness. Is it that a faker chose a feature from a wrong region or style; is it an early alteration; or is it perhaps an original combination of two seemingly unrelated concepts? Often, rural examples originally combined in one piece two or more ideas that have different sources or were used separately in urban, high-style centers. Usually the combination is the joining of features from two or three distinct styles. For example, figure 48 uses a Queen Anne style (1730–1760) back above a William and Mary style (1700–1735) bannister-back base.

If you know bannister-back chairs (figures 40 and 41), you will find figure 39 surprising. Is it faked up to be rare, or is it a dramatic combination of two styles? No. Figure 39 is a "complete" bannister-back with a Queen Anne splat. Not even the back posts above the seat were altered to the new taste with its reverse-curve shapes (figure 48); rather, a bannister-back bilateral emphasis is strongly maintained by finials above turned back posts. Probably the same man made figures 39, 40, and 41, for they all use double ball turnings on the front legs and back posts, and similar finials: an urn supporting a flattened ball form. The first two use a loose barrel turning on the back posts just below the crest rail, and the third uses this as a central accent on its front stretchers; the first two have sausage-turned front stretchers. Figure 41 is traditional in using the form of the back posts as the shape for the central back members. (These were made by turning two extra units like the back posts, cutting them in half, and putting their flat faces forward.) Figure 40 uses four simple vertical slats with molded front faces—an idea associated with eastern Connecticut and Rhode Island. Other related chairs use either the turned or slat bannisters.

Figure 39 is the only one of the group known to have a Queen Anne splat. One must ask, therefore, whether it is original; were there once bannisters? No, because there are no mortise holes in the original crest rail, or rail above the seat, to hold them; there is only one slot in each, and they hold the splat. Also, the splat has the same traces of original black paint as the rest of the chair, and it has a special and appropriate movement. Most Queen Anne splats are baluster-shaped (figure 48), but that of figure 39 has a central area that is distinctly circular, a round form that is related to the much-used ball turnings of the posts. Its roundness may result from that area having been laid out with a compass. When first viewed, it is possible to see this chair as an odd and perhaps ungainly, over-complex primitive Queen Anne chair. But once perceived as a bannister back with an "updating" splat, it makes sense: It becomes amusing, intriguing, and very desirable.

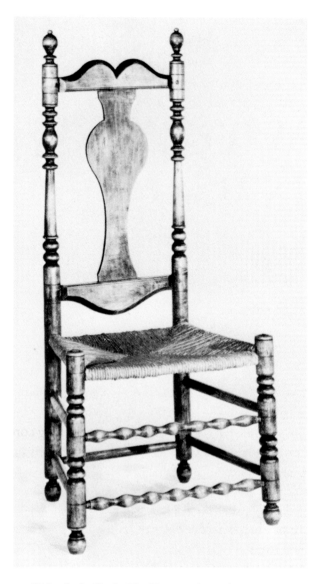

39. Side chair. Probably Connecticut, Avon-Wethersfield area, but similar double-ball and sausage turnings, and the use of four similarly turned feet, appeared in the lower Hudson Valley and New Jersey on chairs whose source-influence was the Low Countries, where this form of foot was popular. (John T. Kirk, "Sources of some American regional furniture," Antiques, 87 [December 1965], p. 798.) 1730–1780. Privately owned.

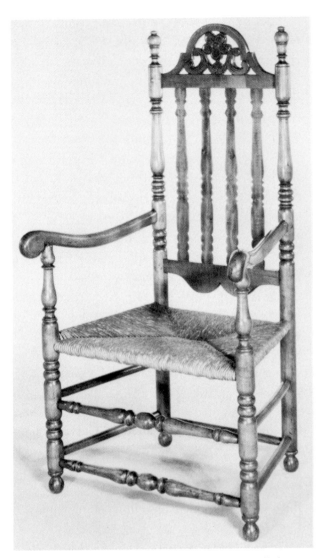

40. *Side chair. See caption of figure 39. 1710–1800. Courtesy, Yale University Art Gallery; The Mabel Brady Garvan Collection.*

41. *Arm chair. See caption of figure 39. All feet replaced. 1710–1800. Courtesy, Yale University Art Gallery; The Mabel Brady Garvan Collection.*

When found, this piece was painted with white enamel and, unfortunately, in cleaning it the lower coat—the original black paint—was mostly removed. In getting off the paint, the depressions (the most recessed parts of the turnings) were given more attention than the rest of the chair when they should have had the least. On an untouched chair, the hollows, which would never have been rubbed, are dark, and the projecting parts lightened through dusting and normal wear. Here, highlights were made of the areas that recede, and the projecting parts were left darker with traces of black paint. To correct this false visual statement, new black paint was rubbed into the depressions so that there now is black in the areas where it should not have worn away. Such repainting, when there is evidence for it, is perfectly legitimate, but one should cover oneself by taking photographs to document such changes.

I have seen it suggested that an object similar to figure 42 should be called a "Carver" chair— a form of stick or turned chair made in the seventeenth century, 1640–1680, with heavy turned posts and elaborately turned spindles in the back. But how would *you* date that chair? What kind of sense can you make out of it? It really becomes very simple if you see it as basically a bannister-back chair: turned back posts with baluster forms, and a double baluster and central ring-turned front stretcher. On this there is a Chippendale crest rail: projecting, or slightly projecting ears—upper outer corners—and a slight arch in the center (figure 43). Then there are six Windsor chair spokes in the back. This is not, as some have felt, a funny object with no source, and to be understood it need not be slipped back into the seventeenth century, where it certainly does not fit. It is an ingenious and intriguing composite of three chair ideas usually seen separately in the second half of the eighteenth century. There is no obvious relationship

42. Side chair. New England. 1755–1820. Privately owned.

43. Side chair. Massachusetts, Boston area. 1755–1795. Courtesy, Israel Sack, Inc., New York City.

44. Stand. New England. Nineteenth century. Privately owned.

45. Stand. Massachusetts, Boston-Salem area. 1800–1820. Courtesy, Israel Sack, Inc., New York City.

between spokes and flanking back posts, which there would be in a bannister-back chair with turned back members; but they are not totally incongruous, for they swell near the base as do the flanking baluster turnings. This is a charming object, which tells us a good deal about primitive design that can use a combination of three different chair ideas. As always, such a piece *must* be dated by its latest feature, the Chippendale crest rail, which puts it *after* 1755. Possibly it is as late as 1800, or it may have been made in the early nineteenth century when light, stick chairs were fashionable.

The primitive stand, figure 44, is also strange. It has legs whittled to octagonal cross-sections; the corners of the legs have been cut away, probably with a rather inadequately used plane, or with a drawknife. The side rails, between the square tops of the legs, are not joined into the legs with the usually standard mortise and tenon joint. (The rail ends are usually cut to tongue extensions [tenons], which fit into holes [mortises] in the legs; then, in most examples, they are pinned into position [figure 105].) Here there are no tenons; in fact, there are no joints involving carpentry; instead, nails are used. The nails are driven from one side of a leg into the end of the skirt that butts onto the opposite side. Both the placing and appearance of the nails suggest pegs until you tap them and hear metal. The top is secured by similar nails driven through from above into the skirt rails below. The nails are late, rectangular-headed cut ones and suggest a date well into the nineteenth century.

The top of the piece had a life before being used on a stand: not only does it have a big gap at one end where a knot has fallen out before it was painted, but it also has knife marks on its under side, which indicate that it was once a cutting board. Yet this board is the only top the stand has had. Each part has only one coat of paint, a medium red-brown, which is consistent on top and base. Additional proof that this is the original top is provided by the fact that there are no unused nail or pin holes in the top edges of the rails and legs which would be there if a different top was once attached. (One way of seeing if a top belongs to a base is to lift it slightly to check if there are marks in the top of the skirt or legs from earlier pins, nails, or screws. It would be almost impossible for anyone adding a later top to get the pins, nails, or screws into the same holes as were used for an earlier top. Only a top-flight faker would attempt this. Usually it is possible to tap up the top, having put a thin board or shingle where you are about to hammer, of course! A similar protective board should be used when you tap the top back into place.)

The thin octagonal legs with the deep skirt above are really quite amusing and make sense only when we see the whole object as a very primitive attempt at something like figure 45, where the legs were first straight-turned and then reeded; and such a deep skirt would only be appropriate on a high-style piece if it held a drawer. On figure 44 it adds the charm of being inconsistent with the slender legs. Also, the broad overhang of the top would not be found in pieces from the major style centers; this is a carry-over from an earlier period.

The stand has the integrity of a farm-made object, and is, like many other primitives, a personal statement. An attempt at rounded legs was made but the maker must have liked what he produced, for the faceted shapes could have been eliminated—the maker could have rendered them rounder by cutting away the eight corners—instead, he left them and had a new personal design. Without the ability or perhaps even the knowledge of mortise and tenon joints, he made his table regardless; and whether he realized it or not, his nailheads look like the pins we expect to find securing mortise and tenon joints if they are there. He was without a lathe, and he cer-

tainly did not have much training. He could not, against much competition, have made a living producing furniture, but he did make something that was wanted and needed, and in such a way that it was not just useful; he went far beyond that and tried to make it beautiful, so that it would please his eye. This and figure 86 were recently purchased in a shop where they had been overlooked by customer after customer. They were too odd, too unusual, too "crude." The stand did not fit into any known slot of stand forms; certainly it was not on anybody's checklist. The proprietor, who likes such things, was amazed that at last a customer understood these two beat-up, direct, unrestored pieces of American art.

The chair, figure 46, can naïvely be seen as a great design leap from the Windsor chair form to modern ideas of far-flung members such as is found in the modern Danish designs of Hans Wegner, particularly his popular "peacock-back" chair. We can say, "What an extraordinary sense of design and use of space," but if we recognize that there were at least two uses for such chairs, they no longer seem an unprecedented leap into futuristic forms. Rather, this becomes a practical object made to suit particular needs. It should be remembered that when one had to go to a cabinetmaker it was not as strange to have variants made as it is today, when hundreds of similar shops sell the same things over and over again. At the time this Windsor chair was made —which would be after 1800, when bamboo movement and oval-shaped unsaddled seats were fashionable—it was customary to drape a cloth or shawl on a high-back stick chair, or to fix around it a fitted cloth. As with a wing or upholstered chair, this kept drafts from the sitter's back and formed a useful guard when the only source of heat, fires, necessarily pulled oxygen, and thus cold air, from outside (during a New England winter such air would chill the

46. *Chair. Probably New England. 1810–1850. Courtesy, Shelburne Museum, Inc.*

most healthy). To keep the cold off one's back various other items were developed, including chair-tables with big tops that tipped up to screen the back, and settles. This chair should be seen with its back draped, or tightly fitted with openings left to allow the sitter's elbows to rest on the rails provided. Also, such chairs were used for invalids; an incompetent could be tied in and firmly secured. There were even adult-sized cradles, some of them with holes or knobs to hold the ropes employed to tie in the mad. The awareness of such uses for unfamiliar forms enables us to see an apparently "unique" object as a rational solution to a problem faced at home when there were few outside institutions. This knowledge does not diminish the object; it can be appreciated for what it is, a culture's solution to a problem.

Figure 47 presents a different problem. At first glance it does seem a legitimate Queen Anne arm chair like figure 48 with rockers added, and, therefore, the price would be high. Figure 48—a straightforward New England primitive Queen Anne chair—was made after 1730, when the Queen Anne style was introduced. The nature of this style is the continuous use of the reverse curve, as can be seen down the edges of the back splat. In a high-style piece (figure 49), there would be an echoing of these curves throughout the entire object; the legs would also have reverse-curve, cabriole shapes that might be re-used in shaping the seat. In primitive objects such as figure 48, often only the back is updated to the new style, for that is the area you are going to see most, while the base continues to use the William and Mary style of baluster- and block-turned legs, with a double baluster and central ring-turned front stretcher. Such a base was continued on later chairs because it was quickly lathe-turned rather than laboriously carved out, and therefore much cheaper. In rural areas, always conservative, it is not surprising to find

47. *Arm chair. New England; possibly Rhode Island. For date see text. Courtesy, Slater Mill Historic Site.*

48. *Arm chair. New England; possibly Massachusetts. 1730–1800. Courtesy, Yale University Art Gallery; The Mabel Brady Garvan Collection.*

49. *Side chair. Philadelphia. 1740–1760. Courtesy, Israel Sack, Inc., New York City.*

this mixture of styles, especially when economics reinforced the wisdom of keeping a tried and trusted strong lower section.

The back of figure 48 has the typical Queen Anne proportions of tall, vertical orientation. Figure 47 seems at first to have the same features, but when scrutinized it is seen to be different. First, there are the rockers. Although rockers were introduced in the second half of the eighteenth century, they did not gain popularity until the early nineteenth, 1820–1830, when they were stuck on to all kinds of old as well as new chairs. Rockers made old chairs more comfortable since the back could be tilted; in addition, they fit with the new fashion. It is easy to see that these rockers were added, for they are so foreign to the forms above them and placed so near to the side stretchers. In fact, we *know* they are later because they do not have as many coats of paint as the legs.

When we move to the back we see something else that puzzles us. The crest rail slightly overhangs the back posts. On figure 48, the outer and inner lines up the back posts flow into the crest rail. The projection of the crest rail on figure 47 should be seen as a later feature, being part of the style that followed the Queen Anne, the Chippendale style, which began in America about 1755, and that typically had crest rails with projecting ears and pierced splats (figure 43). Here the splat is solid. Is it then a Queen Anne chair with a Chippendale crest rail and later rockers? Well, is the splat really Queen Anne in movement? No, its outline wobbles in a manner not typical of the Queen Anne style. A New England Queen Anne splat should relate to that of figure 48, which uses the standard baluster shape with sides made up of long reverse curves. It is the inverted shape of the turned baluster form under the arm, on the top of the front posts. In figure 47, the splat not only wobbles; it pushes its greatest mass down toward the rail that supports it. This is

completely foreign to either the Queen Anne or the Chippendale splat, both of which push the action up toward the crest rail. The splat of figure 47 should in fact jump out as being non-Queen Anne in time and taste.

Apart from the splat, the proportions of the back are wrong: the tall, vertical movement of figures 48 and 49 is missing, *and* the back posts do not really fit the crest rail. The right-hand back post is slightly broader than the area shaped to match it above; the post has been shaved to make a better fit. We must accept that the back of this chair has been altered: the splat has been changed and the crest rail lowered. But when was this done, and how does it affect the chair's importance? Such changes would not be made by a faker. Even if the tops of the back posts had been damaged and lowering the crest rail was preferred to piercing them, a good faker would know what shape the splat should be. It seems proper to assume that all the alterations— the rockers and splat, the lowering of the crest rail—occurred at the same time. It is logical to assume this, but it may not be the case.

How does one decide? First, one looks at the shapes of the new parts, the rockers and splat. Both *look* like the same period. Rockers that became popular in the early nineteenth century had this deep shaping, and the movement of the splat resembles some early-nineteenth-century "fiddle" splats in having the greater mass down rather than up. The unusual form of the crest rail needs explanation, as it lacks the strongly projecting ears one expects. It is in fact a rare form, with its slightly arching outer top edges either side of a central flattish curve. This is a form widely used on simple English and Irish chairs, but it is known only on a few American chairs. It appears on a Southern, possibly Virginia, chair and on a set of Rhode Island chairs once used in Providence by John Brown. The set suggests a Rhode Island origin for this New

England chair. The use of a Chippendale-period crest rail suggests that the chair originally had a pierced splat, but it may have been solid; sometimes only the crest rail was of the latest style, and the John Brown set of chairs* with this crest rail have solid splats.

So what is figure 47? We have an absolutely first-rate chair with fine scrolled arms, and exciting turnings; just compare the boldness of the turnings of the front stretcher with those of figure 48. It has a deep green color (discussed in Chapter 11). The feet are missing, probably taken off when the rockers were added, but those on figure 48 are not original; such chairs were often cut down by people who wanted the seat nearer the floor. Some collectors feel that missing feet need to be restored; fakers add them to get the price of a "complete" piece. On some of these chairs the original front feet are simple baluster-turned forms, repeating the shape of the turnings used above, rather as on figure 125.

* The Southern chair—see John T. Kirk, *American Chairs: Queen Anne and Chippendale* (New York: Alfred A. Knopf, 1972), figure 207. The John Brown chairs are owned by Norman Herreshoff, Bristol, Rhode Island.

Most collectors prefer a chair with Spanish feet, and will pay much more for such a piece. To meet this desire, some fakers cut off the *original* turned feet and put on new, elaborate carved ones. It is now impossible to know if figure 48 originally had turned feet or carved Spanish feet. The presence of rockers on figure 47 does not diminish it any more than the new feet on the second chair. Its lowered crest rail and redesigned splat make the chair intriguing, once understood. Of course it should not be priced as a great, intact Queen Anne primitive chair, but it certainly should be more valuable than an untouched third-rate one.

Once you perceive unusual combinations— whether original or resulting from changes—it often adds to the fun of collecting because you can purchase pieces which most people will not understand. They may, of course, be legitimately laughing at you because you have just bought a fake; but a creative, knowledgeable collector can appreciate and delight in the variant, and fortunately these pieces are usually still much cheaper than the straightforward interpretation of a form. Since they do not fit into what the books say is correct, they are not on most collector's "want-lists."

5

Quality of Design— Comparisons

Quality of design—an object's superior aesthetic impact—is a dangerous thing to talk about because it immediately carries with it the idea of snobbishness, of looking down one's nose like an Olympian god condemning and choosing. People in a democracy like to see value in all things. They like the phrases "beauty is in the eye of the beholder," meaning that everything has aesthetic merit if properly viewed, and "beauty is only skin deep." The first is not true and the second is true only of human beings and early furniture. Beauty is not an attribute brought to the object by the observer; it either is or is not present in the object itself, and if present it was put there by the maker. It comes from the eye and skill of the maker and the wishes of his patron.

Much American furniture is just dreadful. It never was beautiful, and it has not become so with the passage of time. Some of the bad is intriguing as it reveals particular earlier cultural patterns and their aesthetic limitations; some that was bad is now interesting because of what

has happened to it; but the truly beautiful is scarce. Just as most modern designers fall short of the highest standards, so did most early furniture makers. Fortunately for us there was in each early style period, in each region, and at each cultural level, a general concept that kept the constructional and aesthetic level high. A strong tradition existed as to how an object should be made and how it should look.

It is not snobbish to discern the differences between two similar objects, the quality of their designs. To look at an object one must first understand its original concept and purpose. The second step is to understand what was available to achieve this: the means of construction and the general features associated with that form. Next one must evaluate the designer-maker's balance of masses, drawing and execution of line, and choice, arrangement, and execution of motifs available in his region of America. Then it is possible to compare two similar objects to see which reaches a higher level. The genius of the designer-maker is not what he invented, it is his ability to select among what was available and his use of it. In seventeenth- and eighteenth-century America, such choices were very limited. There were very few basic forms, few popular shapes, and few ideas about how to decorate them, whether by shaping, lathe turning, carving, veneer, or paint. In the nineteenth century, a greater variety of choices arose because of the new technology and the revival of earlier styles, but this did not change the designer's role or his approach to an object, it just made it more complex.

The genius of creation lies first in the way in which a designer deals with outside demands—the standard height of a writing surface; the height and width of a large piece so that it scales into the room where it is to be seen; his interpretation of the popular proportions of the time in the general mass. Then he will have to make fundamental decisions as to how to shape his basic line, the line intrinsic to his form—the splat of a chair, the movement of a cornice, the shape of a cabriole leg—and then how to repeat and echo that line elsewhere. Next, he must choose the decoration and decide on its location so that it relates to and enhances the basic underlying shapes. Most exciting to me is to find a simple piece in which the maker outdistanced others in understanding the balance of proportions and movement, and the repeat and echo of a simple line, so that he has created elegant simplicity, a directness of form and pattern. It is usually almost exactly like the work of his contemporaries, but it has been done with a great eye.

Tremendously exciting in another way is to see an elaborate Philadelphia Chippendale highboy covered with carving, turnings, brasses, and intricate grain. That too takes a genius, and in some ways a more complex, developed mind and eye. But always I appreciate the ability to draw a beautiful, uninterrupted line. The superbly cut dress, dependent only on line and balance of shape against shape, is far harder to design and make than one with folds, tucks, darts, swags, and other embellishments. It is easy to cover something with a lot of ornamentation which distracts the eye from the fact that the basic underlying concept is weak. In general, this chapter deals with the comparison of objects where one is better than another, though in some instances two or more are equal.

SLANT LID DESKS

Figures 50 to 53 have designs that were popular from about 1800 to about 1850. (Figures 50 and 51 were found in the Daniel Bliss house in rural southeastern Massachusetts in 1969, and probably had been made locally for that house.) In an urban high-style center, square tapered legs would suggest a date of 1790–1810, but in rural areas, shapes so easily made and so appealing in form persisted long after a style had changed in the fashionable places. In a sense these four desks show a revival of the seventeenth-century idea of the desk box on stand or frame. In the intervening eighteenth century, desks tended to be closed in below and that area fitted with drawers, although a few open-base standing desks were made; they appear in paintings of the period, particularly interiors of offices and libraries.

These four desks employ square tapered legs that reach from the desk section to the floor. The first two have long legs that push the desk section high into the air. Such pieces were probably used for writing while standing, a method that was employed early and is still used by some (Winston Churchill wrote his volumes at a standing desk). On figure 50, square tapered legs go up to the top, and the front, back, and two side boards are tenoned into them so that the joining of horizontals and verticals is in one plane; the vertical movement is caught into the horizontal so that the eye can easily move up one

50. *Desk. New England; probably Rehoboth area of Massachusetts. For date and changes see text. Courtesy, Elizabeth D. Kirk.*

51. *Desk. New England; probably Rehoboth area of Massachusetts. 1810–1850. Privately owned.*

leg, across the front, and down the other leg. The open space within these parts is thus nicely enclosed. There is a fine attention to details: a thin molding edges the lower line of the skirt rail and continues across the legs. However, this desk is not as it was when first made, for the molding has some breakage; the legs have been pieced out, or extended, raising it by about a foot; and the ends of the top board are slightly recessed: it is not as long as the slant lid; its ends and rear edge show no paint. This suggests that originally there was a thin board gallery, as on figure 52. The paint is a soft moss green which, although old, cannot be original as it covers the later extensions of the legs and the oval brass that would have been put there by the maker to give a shiny accent. The presence of an oval brass helps to date the desk more exactly than figure 51. It suggests that the desk is not a very late rural expression since the brass must

have been purchased before that shape went out of fashion in urban areas and ceased to be made. Small ovals were used in high-style centers between 1780 and 1820.

How do you evaluate such a piece? The board gallery is gone, the legs have been extended, it has an old, but not original green paint, and the wood around the left hinge of the slant lid has been broken out and that original hinge replaced by a larger, cruder one. To me it is delightful. Certainly the color is beautiful, enhanced by its wear. The extended legs should be left; they are an early alteration since the old paint goes over them, and they are the kind of legitimate change that can add interest and elegance. There is the decision whether to work on the hinge area; I would probably put on a proper hinge and might fill in the missing wood. Then the question remains whether to restore the gallery. Since we do not know the exact form, and since the

52. Desk. New England. 1810–1840. Privately owned.

53. Desk. New England; possibly Chester area of New Hampshire. 1820–1850. Privately owned.

soft, subtly worn green color would be difficult to reproduce (except by one of the good paint fakers), I probably would not do so.

Figure 51 was found in the same building as the preceding piece. Here the side, front, and rear boards of the box section join each other at the corner. The sides are nailed to the upper parts of the legs, which continue inside the box; the front and back boards are nailed to the side boards. This construction recesses the legs behind the plane of the desk section, making it look a bit like a coffin on toothpicks. The creamy yellow color is pleasant but without distinction. A perfectly serviceable object has been made by someone without much sophistication either in construction or aesthetic judgment, although he did put end cleats on the slant lid.

Figure 52 is both well made and well balanced in design. There is a strong repeat of horizontals—the two "drawers" (the top one is not a

drawer but the front of the desk section), the surface of the slant lid, the top, and the raised board gallery. These play against the tapered verticals of the four legs. The brasses on the "drawers" are original back plates for pulls. They are screwed into place and may never have had the large knobs of the same dimension usually found with them. The bottom of the drawer shows hundreds of fingernail marks made by those reaching under to pull it open. The brass plates make four strong circular accents which play against the original red and black painted graining. The balance is fine and the graining strong. The black and red paint is a stylized echo of the elaborate grain patterns of contemporaneous mahogany and rosewood veneers on more expensive pieces. It is hard to fault this piece.

Figure 53 may at first appear to have the same problem as figure 51. It might seem like a large box on too small a base, and despite its strong powder blue paint, the color of worn denim, it could be overlooked. But when studied, it is seen as the work of someone who wanted stretchers for sturdiness while preferring them pushed back where they would be out of the way, making it a desk attached to a frame. The maker paid great attention to details. The "square tapered legs" are not square in cross-section as normally found, but rectangular, wider than they are deep. This means that there is a wider face to relate to the wide front and slant lid of the desk section, and a narrow face when you look at the narrower sides of the frame. The side stretchers are raised far above those at the front and rear so that each side has two horizontal open spaces, whereas the front has one large rectangular open space. The bottom edges of the rails just under the desk section are slightly arched below, giving the piece a slight visual lift. The stretchers are let into the legs with large dovetail joints which are visible under the paint. The maker also provided molded details, and then painted the desk a strong blue, which light, air, and use have faded to a richer color. On the top surface of the slant lid is tacked a thin piece of metal stamped: "CHESTER' N, H," This piece and figure 52 have hinges whose flat surfaces are visible, continuing a seventeenth-century idea of exposing them. Early hinges, however, were nailed onto the surface; these are recessed into it, to be flush with the top surface, and painted over. Figures 50 and 51 follow the later practice of fitting the hinges into the joint between the top board and the slant lid, with only the rounded "hinge" part visible.

How do you choose among these four desks? I think we can dismiss figure 51 for its crudity, which in itself need not be a negative factor but in this instance it neither lends charm nor makes the piece intriguing. Figure 52 is the most sophisticated, but although it is nearest to what was made in a high-style center, it is so in a way that

makes a new personal statement of great charm, rather than being a pale reflection of a more developed piece. Certainly it must be thought of as one of the better primitive pieces made in America shortly after 1800. Figure 50 has been altered to fit new needs as time passed. It is not worth as much as figures 52 and 53 but it has its own integrity. This is a good example of alterations adding to, rather than detracting from, a piece's merits. Figure 53 is more difficult to accept easily because it breaks with tradition by putting a box on recessed legs; but since it does so in a way that creates rather than diminishes interest, it excites more than the others.

Given these four pieces to choose from, all priced the same, I would find it very difficult to decide between figures 52 and 53. My selection would depend on the setting for which I was choosing. If for a period house, then my decision would be based on whether the setting was more or less rural. The determining factor cannot be a question of different dates of manufacture with these particular examples. The large circular brass pull-plates of figure 52 suggest a date of 1810 to 1840, the nails and color of figure 53 much the same time. One difference is that figure 52 will be worth more in the future. It is more likely to be on the "checklist" of most buyers. It is neater, smaller, and more useful— it would fit into more spaces. Smallness has become one of the criteria of the collectable today, when many buyers of early furniture live in apartments. The choice would really be a matter of personal taste, or pocketbook. Figures 52 and 53 are "better," but figure 50 should not be ignored.

TABLES AND TABLE LEGS

The table and three table legs, figures 54 to 57, were all probably made in the first half of the nineteenth century. Figure 54 is distinctly influenced by bamboo turning, as found on the

54. Table. Northern New England; found in North Sandwich, New Hampshire. 1800–1840. Privately owned.

Windsor chair, figure 31, and is perhaps slightly earlier in date than the three following examples, which use turnings found on thousands of tables made from about 1820 onward, perhaps to the end of the nineteenth century. All three, along with figures 50, 51, and 72C, were found in the same house. Together they demonstrate the kind of simple, interesting rural pieces that should, but so rarely do, dominate "restored" country houses. Figure 55 begins with a top section left "square" so that it could receive the rails in a mortise and tenon joint; below it is turned straight, then with a ring, then a long straight, another ring, then a baluster above another baluster; the foot is a tapered ball form. The table has original graining of black lines over a red ground, like figure 52, but it is not as dramatically patterned. Figure 56 has the squared upper part above a straight, two rings, a strong baluster shape, another ring upon a reel; below the reel is a long section whose lower third tapers in slightly to a reel, on a ring above a baluster, which rests on a flattened ball foot. The table has an original coat of red paint, and surprisingly the whole piece is made of pine (the legs of the other tables are of a harder wood).

55.   56.   57.

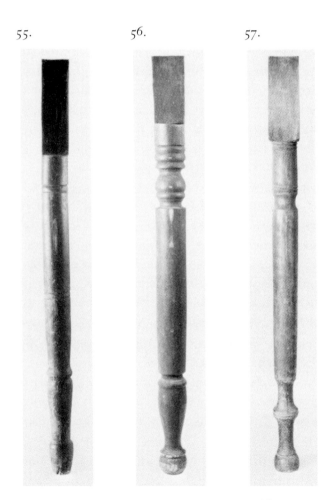

55, 56, 57. Table legs. New England; possibly Rehoboth area of Massachusetts. Nineteenth century. Privately owned.

Figure 57—which is perhaps slightly later than the preceding two—has the square, then two very narrow rings, a straight, and two narrow rings; then a reel form above a long curving taper to a long reel and a ring; then an even longer reel on a flattened ball foot. The table is birch, and the whole has a very thin coat of red paint-stain.

Which of the four do you choose? I immediately go for the first. Perhaps because, with its echo of bamboo shapes, it is earlier in form even if not necessarily in date. Somewhere in the back of my mind the idea keeps nagging me that earliness is better; better because it means older, and therefore rarer. But I think I like it best because of the directness of its design. It is less complex, although simplicity need not be a superior factor. I like the deep clarity and spacing of the two upper reel turnings—one above and one below the stretched-out baluster form of the main part of the leg. And I like the inward curve of the bottom of the leg, where it moves to the lowest reel above the ring foot. And, of course, I like the tiger maple of the leg, and the deliciously worn, heavy pine top. This table was a "sleeper." As I said earlier, it was painted with Chinese red enamel and used with many other tables of less age and interest to support inadequate but elaborately ornamented china and glass; nevertheless, its form was visible to all. It was "discovered," cleansed of the disguising paint, and its merit revealed. It stands apart from the following three legs which use a more standard vocabulary in their turning.

I find figure 57 weak. I want to say it is quiet and pleasant in form, but I think it is probably ill-defined and boring; even the upward-decreasing length of the reel turnings is not really interesting. I like figure 55 because of the paint graining and because of the repeat of the two baluster shapes above the foot, one going out and one going in to produce a gentle vertical movement. Figure 56, because it is turned of pine, which makes large shaping necessary, has a strong directness of form; the design is more "available" to the viewer, and I am intrigued as to what kind of forms the use of softwood implies. I also like its powdery red paint.

BENTWOOD AND BENT METAL CHAIRS

The backs of the two bentwood chairs in figure 58 are virtually the same. Only in the bent leg supports do we see a difference, but it is sufficiently great to change our perception of the whole. Bentwood chairs were brought to a level of sophisticated and conscious art by Michael Thonet during the 1840's in Vienna, and by the beginning of the twentieth century many countries were producing simple versions. They were light, cheap, and very strong. The chair on the right in figure 58 carries on the bottom of its original plywood seat a paper label inscribed: "JACOB & JOSEP . . . [O] H [N or M] . . . / Bentwo[o]d Furniture Fibre[R]ee an[d] . . . ed Furniture / 25 27 West 32nd Street / NEW YORK"; and when looking underneath one sees that the two front legs, the single piece that forms both back legs, and the front and side bent supports, are stamped "34" and "G."

The chair at left has lost its original caned seat, which at one time had upholstery over it, for you can see the tack holes in the top of the seat rail. It was the kind of caning that came in sheets. In the rail is a groove into which the caning was forced by a reed driven downwards to carry the edge of the caning with it. Because one of the chairs is incomplete, it is now more difficult to compare the two designs, for you can see more of the lower structure of one than the other, but this also facilitates inspection. The use on the right chair of four separate and basically similar pieces to brace the legs to the seat makes one's visual experience of the front and sides similar. You follow the legs up from the floor to an arching effect created by the bent supporting

58. *Side chairs. Right New York, left probably American. Early twentieth century. John T. Kirk.*

member. On the sides, the bracing members do go farther down the back legs, giving them additional strength and visual tie-in; but walking around it, one does not experience a real change in one's perception of the chair. On the left chair, there is a similar supporting arch between the back legs. For its other legs, there is one continuous serpentining member, which begins on the front face of one back leg, curves to the seat rail, moves down to join behind one front leg, crosses to the back of the other front leg, then curves up again to the seat rail before plunging to the front of the other back leg. This makes the chair more intriguing as you move around it. The relationship of the supporting member to the seat and legs is continually changing, setting line against line, curve against curve, and the curves of the supporting member, the seat, and

the legs all play against the back. From the front, the recessing of the supporting member behind the front leg makes the seat rail above project toward you. This gives an openness which allows you to move into the design. Your eye is not locked to the front plane as it is in the chair on the right. There the horizontal curve of the seat rail does play against the vertical curve of the supporting member, itself an intriguing relationship, but the chair on the left allows movement into the design which gives a greater sense of space and air, a freedom of entrance into the design.

The bending of material was not new with Thonet, and it was known in metal as well as wood; in the early twentieth century it was widely used in bent metal forms known as ice-cream-parlor chairs. Figure 59, A to C, represents

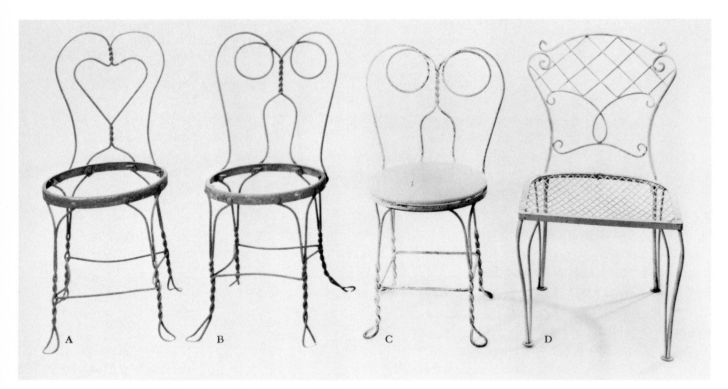

59. *Side chairs. American. For dates see text. Privately owned.*

this group of once-common designs associated with those now-romantic days of ice-cream sodas and other visual wonders served by mustached men in white aprons behind glistening counters. Chairs B and C seem at first to be virtually identical, but C is a new version of the type. It has a broadened and shortened back, and by making the circles in the upper part larger, they have become the dominant shapes, like great owl eyes. The seat is a narrow band of metal with inner flanges, through which screws pass to secure a padded, plastic-covered seat that floats above the iron rail like a great soft peppermint. A leg begins as one metal strand being welded to the inside of the seat; about halfway down it twists, goes on to the floor, loops back on itself, twists around, and goes up to have its other end welded in place. Then a very square, continuous stretcher

is welded inside the four legs, where it looks disparate from all the curving parts.

Chair B, which is much earlier, has a taller, narrower back and none of its areas dominates the design. One member of the front legs is bolted near the center of the seat, then goes not quite halfway down, where it begins to twist around the other member of the front leg; but instead of continuing to the floor, it makes an angle and becomes a stretcher. When it reaches the back leg, it twists around and heads down to make a foot; it then backs up on itself to begin the rear member of the back leg. The other legs do the same: part of them comes out, twists, makes a stretcher, and becomes a member of another leg. No welding was necessary. Not only is this structurally sounder, but every element is visually integrated. One does not read the stretchers as disparate parts, almost afterthoughts added for strength. Similarly, in the back there are rising central members that, after they have finished twisting on themselves, do not return to the same side of the chair from which they originated; the one that begins left of center ends up all the way around to the right of the back. A nice integration of design and construction. To the same effect the heads of the bolts that secure the legs to the seat rail are left visible on the seat rail; the inner part would not, of course, have been seen when a seat was in place.

I wondered, when I first began to write about chairs A and B, whether the stretchers originally curved inward as they do now. Later foot pressure could have done it. However, I recently saw dozens of similar chairs in an ice-cream parlor in Boston and they all appear as here, so the curving must be original as one would have expected in objects so conscious of movement. The seats would have been set into the iron ring with their tops flush with its top line. Chairs A and B have been so used, so pulled across floors that they have feet that have worn through.

Chairs A and B make an interesting comparison. Chair A's stretchers go through, but do not become part of the twisted leg. This is successful because the stretcher seems a part of the leg movement, although it is not as interesting nor as strong as the base of chair B. The back does not have the same exchange from side to side: those members which begin on the right end on the right, and those on the left stay on the left. However, the central heart shape plays against a similar outer curve; this and the narrower stance of the back makes it as exciting as B.

Chair D is far from being a successful object. It has simulation but no success. It makes a pretense at having French or cabriole legs, which are welded to buttons to keep them from entering the ground, for this is an outside or lawn chair. Above, they are welded to a triangular plate which is bolted to the D-shaped seat rail. The seat is of a metal mesh, hidden, I hope, during use by a cushion, for its diamond pattern is completely incongruous with the chair's attempted movement. The diamond is repeated in a larger manner, indeed aggressively so, in the upper part of the back, but again it has no correspondence with the waving curves around it. Below these diamonds is an entwined member that rests on a mustache-like serpentine shape that also seems foreign to the rest and is pushed away from it by the entwining loop above, although it repeats the shape of the top rail. This dreadful object capitalizes on our having learned to like curves and iron furniture, but unfortunately it thinks that more is automatically better.

CUPBOARDS

Figure 60 may at first seem to have a better design than figure 61, for it has fielded or raised panels in its door. A piece with panels is considered desirable, and one with raised panels even more so. Also, on the first cupboard the top and bottom boards are dovetailed to the side boards, and dovetails are thrilling to any collector who knows just about enough to have heard of them. These are usually thought of as proving an early date. They do not. Here the flatness or thinness of the panels, the form of the hinges, and the shape of the nails show it to be nineteenth-century. Figure 61 has a simple board door, no dovetails, and the top projects over the front and sides. Yet it is the more interesting of the two. The sides, the door, and the boards that flank it make strong vertical rectangles; the base of the side and flanking front boards are shaped to reverse curves to make the wonderful feet. The sides use the standard shaping found on six-board chests (figure 36), and this is combined with similar shaping on the front to make a unified corner like the bracket feet on more elaborate pieces (figure 38). In the front, the eye goes up

60. *Cupboard. Northern New England or Canada. Early nineteenth century. Courtesy, Joyce Harpin Charbonneau.*

and around the curve of the foot to the door, across its base, and down the other side. This cupboard retains most of its original purple-red paint, while figure 60 has been fairly well cleaned. It was covered with a later paint, which when scraped off took with it much of the original red. There is paint, but it has a scraped look.

Such cupboards are now classified by most dealers under the awful group name "jelly cupboards," as though all nineteenth-century cupboards were dedicated to jelly as the dietary mainstay. Although it is true that the basements of many early houses now have cupboards holding preserves, most of them were put down there by later generations. A piece like figure 61 might have been in a kitchen or pantry but could also have served in some other part of the house. The piece is simply nailed together and painted red, but it became more than an accumulation or conglomeration of boards because the maker gave it style, presence, and a personal, strong shape—its vertical proportions, the balance of rectangular boards, and the shape of the feet that lift toward a slightly overhanging top.

DRY SINKS

It seems that dry sinks are the passion of every beginning collector. Why, I do not know. At one time in my youth I owned three. Two cost $15.00 each, and one that was fairly well rotted was $12.00. I thought I had captured American furniture. It was recently suggested to me that I write an entire book on dry sinks because, "They're so fascinating, and you can never find one published like the one you're considering for purchase." Well, you are not going to find very many that are like one pictured no matter how many hundreds and thousands are published, because they tended to be individually made; in addition, the idea of writing about one thousand or even one hundred dry sinks would by itself drive me from the field. Also the idea, if it were possible, of choosing a piece because it appears in a book is dangerous.

Serious collectors spend big money on a "published" object, thinking that it protects them against fakes, but the belief that such an object is necessarily good is, of course, ridiculous. If it was published when it was part of a collection and is no longer there, one must ask why. There may be valid reasons. The collection may have been auctioned at the death of the owner, or he may have had financial difficulties; he may have had several similar pieces and decided to keep only the best, or the one that interested him most. But to buy only because it is "published," particularly when it appears in a magazine whose staff not only has no control over what is published, especially as an advertisement, but also may not have seen the item, is just asking for trouble. A museum catalogue by someone with sufficient expertise is a different matter. This gives credence to the object to the degree that the scholar was accurate, and spent enough time studying what he was writing about. But it should be remembered that a published picture is just as available to the faker.

I include two dry sinks because one is charming (figure 63), and anything that is charming is interesting, and because the other demonstrates my opinion that most dry sinks are a bore, particularly when they are as broad, as uninteresting in balance of parts, and as altered and refinished as figure 62. The latter, probably from the Pennsylvania area, has two flat-paneled doors below a recessed top sink. It has been cleaned of later paint to some of its original red. The top edge of the back board has recently been planed or smoothed, suggesting that there was once an arching splash board as found on many related pieces; the rear halves of the tops of the side boards show recent smoothing and nail holes, indicating that something was once attached

61. Cupboard. New England; purchased at "Williams" auction in Rockport, Massachusetts. Early nineteenth century. Privately owned.

62. Dry sink. Pennsylvania area. Nineteenth century. For changes see text. Courtesy, Joyce Harpin Charbonneau.

63. Dry sink. New England. Nineteenth century. Courtesy, Joyce Harpin Charbonneau.

there, perhaps brackets that went up to the missing rear splash board. This missing upper area may have made the sink an interesting form, but now it is just a horizontal box with two doors. Once it functioned as a useful item, and it might be terrific today if it had some interest to its form and a great surface—marvelous paint, color, texture, and wear. At present, it is no different from a piece recently made of old boards; it does not matter artistically; even as a document it shows little about what Pennsylvania-area dry sinks were like. Fortunately, it does lack one feature usually added now to "improve" such pieces. Often the original zinc lining of the sink area is replaced by "prettier" copper. This lacks either.

Figure 63, probably from New England, is charming because of its proportions, the placement of the two little drawers with wooden knobs high up and far out on the front surface, and the way the squarish rectangles of those drawer fronts play against the vertical rectangular shapes of the door and the boards that flank it.

Its light yellowish-gray paint has been nicely worn around the edges. The shrinkage crack under the left bottom corner of the left drawer is proper and the kind of character that should be there. It should *not* be filled in. Unfortunately, the present owner did not like the metal latch used to close the door for it revealed the piece as late-nineteenth-century, and this was removed. It should be put back. Many collectors would prefer figure 62 to figure 63 since it has paneled doors, but as with figures 60 and 61 the "plainer" one has finer line and balance of parts.

STANDS

The three stands, figures 64, 65, and 66, are similar in that they use square tapered legs, skirts holding a drawer enriched with a circular or oval brass, and tops with a narrow overhang. Figure 65 is of tiger maple with various inlays: patterned stringing just above the lower edge of the skirt that continues over the legs; diagonal veneer around the edge of the drawer, just inside cockbeading; and a top with patterned inlay around the edge, as well as a diamond enclosing a circular patera in the center. It is stylish but without the ultimate sophistication of a developed urban high-style piece. Although tiger maple was used in urban centers like Boston, at this date mahogany was the common wood for elaborate pieces. This stand is probably from a less sophisticated center but is by a very fine cabinetmaker. It has style and elegance, and the directness of the finest American furniture of the period—it would bring a high price. It is the kind of piece that the makers of figures 64 and 66 might have known, and it is possible to think of their stands as inferior versions of it.

None of figure 65's sophistication of line is shown in figure 64. Not only is it without inlay but its legs, skirt rail, and top are thick by comparison, and it is painted. Figure 66 is more like figure 65 because it has leaner parts and has had its paint removed to maple-esque (actually it is birch). But really it is not fair to compare these, for figure 64 did not try to be the same thing as figure 65. Instead of being elaborately stylish it was to be a useful, simply made, attractive object; it knew it was not figure 65 and did not attempt to be. What makes it wonderful is the royal blue paint, which practically comes out and shakes hands with you.

What about figure 66? It was more like figure 65, even before its paint was removed. It had lean, perky elegance; it is a shame it is no longer "old." Now there is nothing to make you want to touch it and have it as a part of your life. The boxier, heavier stand, figure 64, has a paint that will be an interesting part of any household with an awareness of color and surface.

BOXES

Collectors are usually tempted to build up a collection by acquiring related objects that will play off against each other and will show that

64. Stand. New England. 1800–1850. Privately owned.

65. Stand. New England; possibly New Hampshire or eastern Massachusetts. 1790–1810. Courtesy, Israel Sack, Inc., New York City.

66. Stand. New England. Purchased in central New Hampshire. 1800–1850. Privately owned.

67. Boxes. American. Nineteenth century. Privately owned.

they have more than one or two of something. This can lead to buying for the sake of similarity rather than quality. The joy of building a collection is to see one worn surface against another, one color against another, and one shape against another, all creating a wonderful surrounding. The simplest way to do this with little money is to buy "unimportant" items that have nice color, surface, and form. Figure 67 shows a small collection of wooden boxes with original surfaces. All but two are painted. Usually such boxes were painted and should still be, for it is their surface and color that makes them different from reproductions. Copies are now available but they lack intriguing and personalized character while often costing more than the simpler untouched early ones.

The boxes exemplify two basic kinds of construction. The simpler is seen in the stack of three at the right and in the open box just in front of them. The top and bottom are circular boards, enclosed by a thin strip held to them by tiny wooden pegs. This thin strip overlaps itself considerably, on these by 3 or 4 inches, and the outer vertical end is secured by nails cleated over on the inside. The second basic construction, seen in the first six boxes from the left, is to point the outer part of the overlapping strip (on tall boxes there are several points). This is perhaps the stronger type, for once you have secured the point of the overlap it tends to avoid the splitting or buckling between nails sometimes found on those with a straight vertical joint (the main part of the widest box just to the right of center). Most boxes have the overlap of the bottom part going in a different direction to that of the lid, perhaps because of the thickness resulting from the overlapping.

Some of the boxes were formed to an oval, as in those at front left. They are rarer, and today more desired and more expensive. Above, at back center, is a late box made for butter and branded with the company's name. It seems never to have been painted. The single oval box at left of front center may have had a very thin coat of paint but now there is just the marvelous patterned dirt from human hands. This is the kind of box which is normally sold as Shaker because it has a pointed overlap, and because that is secured with copper rather than iron nails. At auctions I have seen such boxes refinished to newness with the copper nailheads proudly glistening, looking lovely, just like reproductions (which some of them have been). The widest box is a surprise because the box part has the much-broken vertical joint, and the lid has a very long tapering overlap thinning out to a very long strap. Its battered state makes it too "crude" for most people's taste; but it also makes it cheap, and if it is regarded as an object that has grown distinctive, with a strong and fascinating personality, it can be the focus of a collection.

The three oval boxes stacked at the front left have that nineteenth-century blue that is strong, fascinating, and decorative. The stack of boxes in the back right are variants of green. The lower one has lost almost all its paint through normal wear but what is left is a sea blue-green.

Not only are these objects decorative in color and varied in shape and construction; they are also useful. You can store things in them, from marbles to dressing-table needs—you can hide pads and pencils near the telephone or your secret hoard of chocolates. But more important is their visual usefulness: just a few of them stacked up, or placed in a line, can be dramatic and inter-

esting. If they are chosen for interest of design, wear, and color, they will become valuable. I recently saw in the collection of a famous antique dealer a small circular box about 1½ inches across and 1 inch high; it was painted a dry tomato red color. It was not for sale, but had it been it would have fetched several hundred dollars. It was not the size so much as the fantastic, eye-catching color.

PITCHERS AND JUGS

Figure 68, A to E, shows five brown pitchers. Four are made of red clay; D is of a whitish clay. They are probably nineteenth-century and possibly American. The dealer who sold the two smallest pitchers, A and C, said they may have been made in Boscawen, New Hampshire; but similar shapes and glazes are found in various parts of the United States and Europe. E was purchased in Richmond, Indiana. It was said by the dealer to be a "local product," and he claimed that "The local historical society is interested in it," which is a handy dealer's story that may or may not have been true. But if so, why did they not buy it? It came with a lid of a different color, which probably joined the pitcher after its time of manufacture.

All five pieces have the same basic movement: a large base with a narrower neck above. Three, A, C, and E, have a ring base. The two smaller pitchers move in slightly from it before they swell out. All five have swelling lower parts, but D has a straight vertical in that mass. On each the swelling goes in to a double line that makes a ring before moving into the neck. This is purely decorative, if you can say that of anything with such visual and aesthetic function. It is like the string course, or projecting line of bricks, between the stories of a brick house; it visually stops the eye movement momentarily and gives a horizontal accent where the lower mass is about to move into the upper part. This is essential on such

68. Pitchers. Possibly American. Nineteenth century. Privately owned.

pieces, for otherwise you would have a big bal-looning shape that just flowed up into a neck. The smallest pitcher, C, has no terminating unit at its top edge, while A and E finish in a small ring. The two largest pitchers, B and D, have a broad top band; B uses three incised lines that make the band appear as three units.

The handles move differently on all five pitch-ers and help create the particular visual impact of each. The handle of C has a very sweeping, circular movement that works well with the squat, rounded quality of its main form. If a similar sweeping handle were used on A, it would swing too far into space, so it uses a more vertical one. Each pitcher employs color differently. Part of what makes the center one so wonderful is its dark, rich color. E uses a more mottled glaze; it is the same all over, the whiter parts being light reflections from the paper on which the pitchers sit. (This reflection is also found on the other pitchers and the jugs in figure 69.) B has a drip-

line below its mid-band, its lower glaze is thin and lightly mottled, and the upper one is thick and has brown spots in the greenish-brown base color. D is a rather boring gray-chocolate brown with some dripping, but these few dark streaks are probably not intentional since they are not strik-ing and make no obvious or intriguing pattern. D would be cheaper than B since it is "standard" and lacks a marvelous color and texture. But D has quality of form: the handle is elegant in movement and, being as wide as the lip is deep, makes a visual interest in their relationship. B is more interesting to those seeking rarer, individu-ally made and glazed pieces. D, although cheaper, has great form.

The four redware pieces—figure 69, A to D—were called "Boscawen" by the dealer and said to be from the same factory as A and C in figure 68; but again the form is common throughout the eastern United States as well as Europe. A and B have a form that may come from earlier

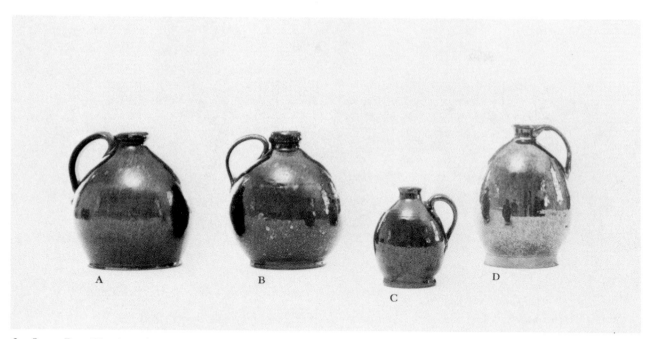

69. *Jugs. Possibly American. Early nineteenth century. Privately owned.*

pieces that were equally round but usually had a longer neck, many of which are inscribed "Sack," an early term for sherry. The one on the left, A, sets its main mass into a base ring and at the top stretches right up into the top rim; B is a purer ball form. The handle of A is bigger in scale and more dramatic. D is a stretched-out version that does not have a capacious roundness of form; it does not say, as A and B seem to, "I contain goodness," and its handle is joined to the top lip, which keeps that part from having a distinct area that can play against the main mass and against the handle. The small size of C is unusual. It has a mottled dark brown color. An expert on pottery who examined it would not commit himself as to whether it is or is not a fake. Its bottom does not show the wear it would have if it had been used, but perhaps it was purely decorative from the beginning and should therefore show no wear. The handle is set farther down from the neck than those on A and B, and it is the

only piece here that has a banded decoration of incised rings about one-fourth of the way down from the top. (This banding is found on the pitchers in figure 68.)

I have purposely not talked about the actual pottery process as a conditioning factor in the design, as I would have done in comparing objects of different materials, made by different processes. Rather, I have accepted that what could be done by one potter could be done by another. This is only true to the degree that each person working in the medium knew everything everyone else knew, both in the actual potting skill and in the awareness of aesthetic possibilities. A maker cannot be criticized for absorbing only those things known and practiced in his area. In judging the pitchers in figure 68, one must be aware of their separation both in date and geography. A and C can be compared because they are sufficiently alike and could be from the same area and period.

70. Tea pots. Left Malden, Massachusetts; stamped by James H. Putnam, working 1830–55. Center and right New England. Second quarter of the nineteenth century. Privately owned.

TEA POTS

The three pewter tea pots in figure 70 are close in date, the second quarter of the nineteenth century.* The pot on the left is the only one with the maker's mark: it is stamped on the bottom "PUTNAM." The pot in the center and the one on the right both use a very dramatic repetition of form. If you cover the lid, spout, and handle, it is easy to see that the upper half of the body simply reverses the lower half. The same mold was used for each half and then the parts were soldered together in the middle. Fascinatingly, this absolute repeat does not produce boredom, for as you look down on the design (which is the normal angle when looking at a tea pot), the effect of foreshortening and the swelling of the center make the lower half look different. Also, the spout and handle give more visual complexity and movement to the upper half, which

* Charles F. Montgomery, August 1974, in conversation.

the lid carries through further enrichment to the finial. (The finial on the right pot has been replaced.)

The Putnam pot at the left has a more complex design. The upper and lower sections have reel shapes; the upper one is bigger. Below each is a reverse curve made in two parts, the upper reverse curve being broader. The movement of the upper part of the pot, and the cleaner movement of its handle, give it the more serene design. Fortunately, the handle of the center pot retains some of its original black paint used to suggest the ebony handles found on silver tea pots. The lids of the three pots make an interesting comparison. The center one has a large simple dome above a bold quarter round, while the one on the right has a smaller serpentined dome above a cove shape, and the one on the left an even smaller serpentined dome above a two-part serpentine that repeats its foot and recalls the band on the body just above the spout. It is wonderful that these objects could be so different although they were made for much the same purpose, at much the same date, in possibly the same region of America, for people who were probably much alike.

CANDLEHOLDERS

Figures 71 and 72 show, with one exception, iron candleholders which have the nickname "pig scrapers"; indeed, one of these when purchased had the bottom filled with pig hair, and figure 72C has pig hairs stuck in the joint between its upper and lower parts. The tradition is that although these were made as candleholders, they were also used for the removal of pig hair after slaughter because their lower edge could be sharpened, their rounded shape was particularly suitable for the job, and the upper shaft made a good handle. (I have seen similar round bases with a wooden handle instead of an iron shaft, and photographs of pieces with rounded "bases" at each end of a metal shaft.) I have heard this story elaborated to the point where not only was the base good for scraping and the shaft for holding, but it was also possible to have a candle burning when you worked in the dark!

It is also a tradition that these are Shaker-made, and if not Shaker, certainly American. The two candleholders in figure 71 were purchased in London and are English, and candleholders similar to those in figure 72 are found in quantity in England. Some of these carry an abbreviation for Birmingham (England) on the upper face of the lip that sticks out at the base of the plunger. With the lip you could push up the plunger to expel used candles. The brass candleholder, figure 72A, was also purchased in England and has a brass ring above its middle, or the remains thereof, similar to the brass ring on the iron candleholder near it. It also has the hook from the top flange, which could be used to hang it over something like the slat of a slat-

71. *Candleholders. English. Late eighteenth or early nineteenth century. Privately owned.*

back chair so that the candle could give light for reading or other work. It is not unusual to find burnt areas on the bottom of slats, undoubtedly from such candleholders having been hung from a lower slat.

The majestic candleholders in figure 71 might at first appear to be a pair, but actually they are very different. The one on the left has a greater arch to its base; the flange that moves from that base to the shaft is a quarter-round shape (on the other candleholder the flange is serpentine-shaped); the extended part, or lip, of the plunger is larger and heart-shaped. The one on the left is 12¼ inches, about ¼ inch taller than the one on the right. This is not because the shaft is longer but mostly because the top flange angles up and out, while the one on the right is serpentine-shaped and moves slightly down. It might be difficult to choose between these two candleholders, yet to me the one on the left has greater drama of movement. From the surface on which it sits, the base angles up sharply to its dome,

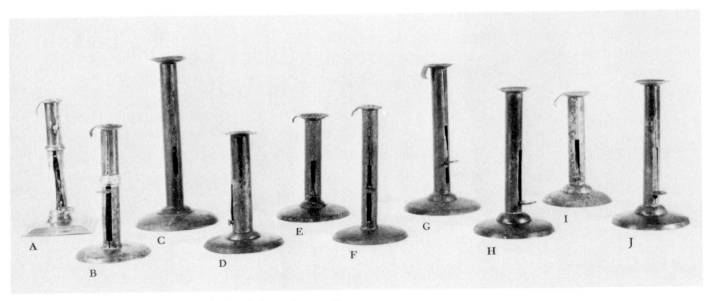

72. *Candleholders. Mostly English, perhaps a few American and Canadian. Late eighteenth and nineteenth centuries. Privately owned.*

whose movement brings you the simple arching of the quarter-round flange; from there you go up the shaft to the top flange, and then out. It is simpler, while also bolder. These large pieces do not have a hook to hold them on a slat-back chair. Undoubtedly, they had a more prominent station. A similarly large one was used in a tavern in Providence, Rhode Island, according to the label on it at The Rhode Island Historical Society.

The ten candleholders in figure 72 show the variations possible within what might seem a standard form. Two, H and J, were bought as a pair, but were they originally so? There is a small difference in the lift from the surface on which they sit to the arched base. J has a small broken-away area in the top flange, suggesting that a hook was once present, while there is no such evidence on the other. H is stamped with a name on the top of the projecting lip of the plunger, just discernible as "SHAW." These variations could have been the work of the same man mak-

ing two different objects, but the plunger lip of H is a separate piece stuck into the vertical part of the plunger, while the plunger lip of J is an extension of the plunger itself, bent out at a right angle. The constructional variations combined with aesthetic differences suggest that the dealer presented them as a pair while they were not originally so. They do look fine together, but a "pair price," always higher, was not justified.

The other candleholders show further variations. The main shaft of F, also stamped "SHAW" on its plunger lip, is thinner, and it and B share a construction different from the others. The rest have a lower quarter-round flange that is part of the shaft; together they make an upper part which is bolted through the domed base—the projecting bolt and its nut are visible from below. The two "variants" both have a shaft with two extensions which penetrate two similarly curved slits in the base; these are clinched over below. It is interesting that the two SHAW pieces, F and J, use differing means of joining the parts, show-

73. Candleholders. European; possibly Portuguese. Seventeenth century. Privately owned.

ing that one maker *may* use a variety of constructions. But, Shaw may only have stamped them as seller, not as maker.

The iron candleholder, C, was found in the Daniel Bliss house and was undoubtedly part of its early furnishings. The flange between shaft and base has an extra line or depression, unlike the simple arching quarter round found on the others. It has a small break in the upper flange which suggests there was a hook, and the lip of the plunger is missing; originally, it was a separate piece screwed into the plunger shaft and not just a bent-up extension of it. Most of these objects seem always to have been a black-brown resulting from the heat, but D and I seem once to have been shiny. D has an old screw as the plunger's lip, which may have been added later. Other differences are in the proportions: height, and sometimes the width of the shaft and base. Each is sufficiently interesting so that personal taste alone will determine which will interest you most.

The seventeenth-century European (possibly Portuguese*) brass candleholders, figure 73, again offer a personal choice. They are very much the same, yet each deserves individual appreciation. The one on the right has parts which are easily read as separate units placed in conjunction that build up to a fine total form. Starting at the surface on which it sits, there is a cove, or inward curve, to a little ring or quarter round before the broad, slightly inward-tapering vertical that brings you to the main top plate (the wax-catching part). This has a ring-decorated edge. Its main mass dishes down and in to the small serpentine shape that brings you to the second part, the vertical shaft, which was cast separately and threaded into place. (The upper shaft is solid; the lower is hollow and open below. Many such candleholders are now the combination of two old pieces—originally parts of different objects—that have been combined or "married" in modern times to make up one "complete" piece.) The vertical shaft has two and a half reel shapes, which lead directly to a form that at first seems like a ball; but its lower part is slightly tapered, while its main mass is in the upper part; this moves to a reel shape. The upper edge of the reel shape flares to the candle-holding section, which is nearly 2 inches tall. Its base is a ring, and then there is a tiny quarter round, below a slightly outward-tapering straight section pierced to create two holes. The use of holes preceded the plunger as a means of extruding the stub of a candle. Then at the top there is a slightly downward-leaning ring. The final form is very strong and the upward movement consists of a series of strong horizontal accents.

The holder on the left is very different. It builds from the bottom with two stepped arching shapes rather than commencing with a gently moving cove. The main wax-catching plate,

* Charles F. Montgomery, August 1974, in conversation.

the top of the base, is flat although it seems slightly arched because of its rounded outer and rising inner edges. The main part of the shaft has long reel turnings, and the "ball" form is a baluster shape with a strongly tapering base. Above it, the straight shaft is shorter. The entire piece integrates upward orientation and is more easily seen as a unified design. I like the candleholder on the left because I think it is a better design. But I prefer the one on the right because of its boldness, directness, and immediacy of form. So we are again left with a personal choice, which is where we should be when we are talking about things of high quality.

BLOWN GLASSES

Figure 74, A to K, is to me sheer delight. It presents the kind of problem that can intrigue me, and fortunately some of my friends, for hours. Here is an array of eleven blown glasses that may be American or English; there probably are some of each. Glass A has long been owned by a family that has lived 20 miles west of Philadelphia, Pennsylvania, since the eighteenth century. The glass is said to have descended in

the family since its initial purchase, which would probably have been in the beginning of the nineteenth century, 1800 to 1830. Several of the other glasses were purchased from a genuine farm sale in central New Hampshire. (Many farm sales are not what they appear but may have a few items from the farm while the rest are brought in by the auctioneer.) Related glasses are reported as having been manufactured in eastern Massachusetts early in the nineteenth century, and similar glasses are found in England, and probably Ireland, so it is difficult to know where these were made.

Since they are, as English guides seem to insist upon saying of anything that is early, "Handmade by hand," there are infinite variations. The tallest glass, B, is 4 1/8 or 4 3/16 inches high, depending on whether you measure the high or low side. The shortest is C, which is 3 7/8 inches high on its tallest side. J and K show the basic, classic ways of treating the stem. J goes from the foot to a quarter round, then in a reel shape swings to a ring, placed at the center of the stem, with a pointed edge. Then it swings in and out again in another reel shape, flaring to support the

74. *Glasses. Probably some English and some American. Early nineteenth century. Privately owned.*

base of the hollow part. This is flowing line. K has a strong central column connecting the base to the top part, with a medial blunt ring accent; it is an arrangement of verticals and horizontals. These two stems show the same differences in design attitude as the preceding brass candle-holders. The other glasses show variants of these two movements. I am particularly fond of D, which raises the ring accent two-thirds up the shaft; the flow of A, with its two strong reel shapes, is also fine. The two glasses, A and B, make a good comparison. The bases of the upper hollow parts are cut to facets. B has a folded foot—when it was hot the base was extended much more widely, and the outer thin edge was bent under so that the present outer edge is doubled. This is considered much better by collectors, but the glass with the Pennsylvania history, A, has much better shaping to its stem. If you are buying form you would choose this one; if you are buying the "collectable," you would choose B.

An interesting note on the problem of relying on family histories, as to when or where a piece was made, is that the present owner has several

times, without realizing it, transferred the Pennsylvania history from the glass without the folded foot to the one with the folded foot, since the latter is more desirable. It is very easy to juggle histories about, unconsciously linking them to the object which seems to deserve it more. All these glasses are interesting. They are somewhat although not extremely rare, and to choose between them is to choose a combination of good and bad features, since each can be faulted in some area. One is not completely superior.

The responsibility of any viewer is to have trained his eye to the same level of perceiving balance of mass and decoration, and movement of line, as the great designers achieved in order to create superior pieces. It is possible to learn the cultural factors that influenced a piece: when, where, and why, but all of this comes from outside, and anyone can master it. The most important, and ultimate, step places the responsibility squarely with the viewer. Does he or she have the eye to perceive what the designer put there? Only then is it possible to judge the success of one creation over another.

6

Quality of Design— Sheer Line

There are styles, or periods of taste, that have as their fundamental feature the use of almost unornamented line. Sometimes it is a straight line or series of them (figures 77, 78, and 84), sometimes curved ones. The latter is best known in America in the Queen Anne style of 1730 to 1760 (figure 49) and the late-nineteenth-century Art Nouveau. In the twentieth century, pieces like Saarinen's white plastic chair and table again use plain sweeping lines in the versatile new material, plastic, that makes possible what was before impracticable—light forms capable of sweeping out into space. Most cannot afford, and few want, developed Queen Anne, and even authentic Saarinen is expensive, but that does not diminish the importance of understanding line, for within each style, even when that style is known for its more elaborately decorated versions, there are pieces that depend almost solely on line for their beauty. Mid-nineteenth-century Victorian furniture is thought of as dripping with carved fruit and flowers, but those who made the elaborate also made plain, sheer-line

pieces, and even the decorated have an underlying simple line that is the heart of the design.

Line is one of the basic tools of the designer. It is much of what makes us experience what we see in a piece. A clever designer can use it to make us perceive whatever he wishes. Figures 75 and 76 show two plastic chairs that use almost the same shape for their plastic top, or seating part. These *look* different because of what the designers have done to the bases, both of which are metal. Figure 75 begins at the floor in a circular shape, and with a reel movement—like the reel in the leg turning of early Windsors (figure 26) and the stem of the glass in figure 74A— brings the eye in an inward-curving line to the seat. Its in and up sweeping curve, makes the upper part seem to float in space. (On an original Saarinen chair the upper part of the reel would flow out to visually support the seat even more.) The metal legs of figure 76 draw a rectangular space below the seat making the upper part sit firmly on a strongly delineated squared space.

75. *Chair. Marked:* NORTH CENTRAL INDUSTRIES, INC / JOHNSON CREEK, WIS / PATENT PENDING / NO. 12306. *Third quarter of the twentieth century. Courtesy, WGBH, Boston.*

76. *Chair. Marked:* A ROBIN DAY DESIGN / MADE IN USA BY / JOHN / STUART / INC. NEW YORK / LICENSED BY HILLE OF LONDON. *Third quarter of the twentieth century. Courtesy, WGBH, Boston.*

There is no floating; the upper part seems fixed to the floor. Actually, less metal is used in this base, but the manner of its use creates greater visual and structural solidity. When, however, you move to the side, you see that the metal legs come together just under the seat to form the upper point of a triangle: from the side, the seat *seems* perched and less stable.

We are constantly acted on by designers and we should recognize this, for awareness is the first step in perceiving what is being done to us; then and only then can we make choices among what is being presented. It is always helpful when we are considering a piece to have something next to it that is almost the same, particularly if one of the two is known to be of high quality. This makes us hone in on similarities and differences, it focuses our eyes and mind, our complete attention, on what makes one piece better. The horrible moment comes if we decide we must have

77. Stool. New England; purchased in central New Hampshire. Nineteenth century. Privately owned.

both! Of course there are times when we should, but there are more when we should have neither. My personal philosophy is, "If you can walk away from it, do so."

Each of the next six illustrations stands alone because each should be recognized without a lesser companion as something of real interest. Figure 77 is a simple stool that could have been made any time in the nineteenth or perhaps early twentieth century. There is no "decoration," just four plain turned legs or corner posts, two stretchers to each side, and four rails holding the original splint seat. There is an original thin coat of gray paint. The stool is narrower across the back than the front, so it is like a tall chair seat without a back. It is the kind of object that should not cost too much. One might think that hundreds of such pieces exist, and that they were made to go with high desks such as figures 50 and 51; but such forms are rare and vary greatly in quality. Important in such simple designs is the balance between the parts: the relationship of the thickness of the legs and the stretchers; the shapes of the rectangles created by the legs, stretchers, and seat rails. These rectangles are significant, for as you walk around the piece they play one against the other; each changes in relationship to the others. Important also is the presence of the original color and splint seat. Since it is one of the simplest pieces ever made, it is essential that "everything works," for its construction is its design. A lesser man could have made a lesser object. The balance of the thicknesses of the parts could easily have been less well handled—the posts made too thick or too thin for other parts. Nor is this harmony of placement of parts easily achieved. There could have been three or four stretchers in each side producing thin, rectangular open spaces; the absence of a taper to a narrower back would have produced a boxier form.

78. Table. New England; purchased in central New Hampshire. 1800–1850. Privately owned.

Figure 78 is a table with square tapered legs and a cleated end top; the cleats are attached with wooden pegs. The front skirt has a drawer that never had a knob or pull, and the entire piece is painted with a flat medium red paint, which has been scrubbed from the top. The top is secured to the base by four wooden pins that go through it into the tops of the legs. This continues a form of construction found in the earliest pieces but long discontinued in related urban pieces. For the latter, it was standard by this time to use screws which began from inside the skirt rail and angled up through it into the top.

Pieces like figure 78 can be found by the dozen. Most have been refinished to glossy maple or birch bases, with "lovely" pine tops. For some reason these are thought better than reproductions, but it would be preferable to have an accurate copy of figure 78 than an inferior and skinned piece with heavy or spindly legs, and less overhang to the top. Often pieces are praised for having "one-board" tops (this top has two boards), while other features, of greater importance are not commented on. It is like praising an old house simply because it has wide-board floors.

79. Hanging box. New England. Early nineteenth century. Privately owned.

This is an absolutely top-flight object, which uses a simple repetition of rectangles. The legs, with their taper, are not of course pure rectangles but their vertical shape plays against the horizontal rectangle of the skirt rail, which has the inner rectangular repeat of the drawer. This is particularly evident since the drawer never had a pull; such a feature would completely alter the design. The edge of the top board provides the final horizontal slash. As you move in toward the piece, the legs, skirt rail, and drawer recede in importance and the rectangle of the top surface grows to become the dominant feature. This is a fascinating, simple piece that changes continuously as you move around, closer and then back

from it. There is no wasted element. The upward flare of the legs gives lift; it pushes the table's mass up from the floor both physically and visually. The cleated ends that are now so prominent because of the shrinkage of the main boards seem an echo of the legs, although this would not have been nearly so visible before they protruded beyond the edge and the paint was scrubbed away. This table is a straightforward useful object of great quality with a terrific surface.

The three hanging boxes, figures 79 to 81, are also basically line and could easily have fallen short of any interest. On each the area of ornamentation, the part that fascinates the eye, is the top curved unit. These units are decorative, but they exist chiefly to have a hole in them for hanging the object on a nail. They combine function and eye entertainment. Figure 79 was probably for cutlery. There is a small arched top above the hole from which the neck sweeps down and in and then out to the sides that angle down to a narrow front. The action is down this curve and down the angled sides to the front. Each part was simply nailed into place and then the whole was painted a greeny-yellow on which white polka dots create a diagonal pattern much as we saw on the cupboard, figure 2. Absolutely necessary to the success of this piece is both the way the neck narrows in below the hole before it sweeps out to the sides and the dotted decoration. Similar boxes have been sanded to "natural pine" and glossed up with varnish; many of these have been published again and again as great Early American pieces. They are no more "Early American" than an old board sanded to death. Not only is this a wonderful object now, but it tells the need of people to be surrounded by interesting, lively, and exciting decorated things even if they have to make them in a simple, direct way. While the wealthy could live with block and shell furniture made in Newport (figure 1), and be surrounded by elaborately

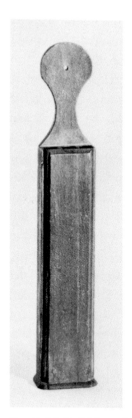

80. (left) Spill box. New England. Early nineteenth century. Privately owned.

81. (center) Hanging cutlery box. American. Mid-nineteenth century. Privately owned.

82. (right) Double sconce. American. Early nineteenth century. Privately owned.

carved and expensively executed pieces, the simpler folk of America could and did create for themselves objects like this. People will make their environment aesthetically interesting. Anyone who came along and diminished such a piece with sandpaper ought to be condemned to a similar fate. (In fact, figure 79 *has* been reworked. The back has broken into many pieces and been re-glued, and the outer surface has been washed after renailing; but the work was done to preserve the paint, not eliminate it.)

Figure 80 has three long, narrow compartments, probably for twisted papers for lighting fires, candles, and pipes. The main area of interest, the place the eye rests, is again the upper

part, which reminds one of the early-twentieth-century painted wooden sculpture of Hans Arp. The front corners of the main box and the base are molded, and the entire surface is painted blue-black.

Figures 81 and 82 show that a similar idea which is satisfying to the eye will appear in various media. Figure 82 is a rare early-nineteenth-century tin double sconce. The arch is stamped with lines to make it possible to bend that part forward, and a series of short straight lines are used to make an inner decorative arch that begins and ends above the candle-holding arms. The inner arch and the outer arch play against each other, as do their arching lines against the circular horizontal movement of the candle cups, which have raying, angled lines that echo those in the top arch. This arch was laid out with a compass whose inner point was the center of what is now the hole for the nail that holds it to the wall: the height from the hole to the top is half of the width of the arch. The top of figure 81 was also laid out with a compass. The arch is 6 inches high and 12 inches wide, giving a very satisfying curve. Many simple pieces were, of course, more casually designed but a number of them when studied are found to be consciously and somewhat complicatedly organized. The bottom front horizontal board of figure 81 is 4 inches high, the opening above it 2½; the middle front horizontal board is 3½ inches high, decreasing by ½ inch from the lower board; the next open space is again 2½, and the top front board is 3 inches high, again a decrease of ½ inch.

Looking for a mathematical logic within a design may seem to diminish its originality, but pieces of furniture were laid out with ruler and compass, and their success or failure lies in *how* the tools were used. If you are going to decrease the board height as you go up, then why not decrease by half inches: 4, 3½, and 3? Since you only need 2½ inches to throw in your knives, forks, and spoons, or whatever you are going to house in these compartments, why not use the same height for both openings? It might be wrong to think that the designer-maker with great sophistication or forethought said, "Let us play a couple of two-and-one-half-inch negative horizontal spaces against three positive horizontal units which diminish by half an inch as we move up." But that *is* what we see; we do not know how much of this was premeditated but we do know that it exists.

The glory of figure 81 is not great age; it is the result of the functional parts being well balanced, and left as the sole decoration—the strong members play against voids and the wall

behind. Like the board cupboard, figure 61, the shaping of functional parts produces the strong decoration. Just as it was not "necessary" to make the shaped bracket feet on the cupboard, so it was not "necessary" to make this arch. It would have been easier to have the back board continue up as a simple long rectangle. That would have taken less work than sawing an arch, and the object would have been just as useful for storing cutlery, but the object was made to serve two functions: use and visual joy. Many related hanging boxes have very simple tops. Others have far fancier ones, and many that started simple are now elaborated by fakers who give them "desirable" shapes such as "fishtails" and pierced "hearts." Figure 81 is not as "collectable" as a more elaborate one and was cheap, but it is extraordinarily fine in its direct use of basic elements with a gloriously arching top section, and it is genuine.

The craftsman's ability to draw a line is part instinct, part training. On a developed piece like figure 1, it is a combination of great eye and elaborate training. In the wooden furniture in this chapter, it is an inborn sense of balancing simple shapes. Few makers have this gift and it is our responsibility to train ourselves to see it when it is there; this is the difference between a useful object and a successful work of art. In fact, line is what we have been discussing all along. The glass pieces in figures 6 and 74 spin line in space; most of the comparisons in Chapter 5 used the movement of basic line as the way of getting at the difference between two or more similar pieces.

So far, line has been discussed as the fundamental underlying factor of a design, but this is not always the way it is used. The basic wooden form of figure 83 is not "sheer line" but its use of paint is. Where figure 37 uses patterned paint as simple surface ornamentation with little sense of movement, figure 83 uses it to make a vividly flowing pattern of great impact. The cupboard was found in Uxbridge, Massachusetts,* and the bottom is signed "Stephen Alb[ier?] / Painter / Sept 4—1840." It is a huge object, really just a giant box with feet formed by a simple shaping, yet its paint makes it a piece of great interest. The base coat is yellow, which is covered with red-purple graining. On most areas this makes simple vertical lines, but on the door the painter has become an exciting artist: the two boards that make the door have "matched grain," one half echoing the other as in elaborately veneered pieces. The possibilities of free movement have been superbly exploited. An interesting and unusual feature is the use on the front of a wider board to the left of the door than to the right. Behind the wider board are two shelves, across the back and at the right one shelf, and below the shelves a line of pegs.

Almost every act of a designer-maker involves line. Whether it is the fabrication of a simple turned part, or the sawing out of a board, line is involved. Then it is the combination of these parts which creates a piece's complex line. How this is handled in elaborate or simple pieces is what makes them either fall short of or achieve greatness.

* Files of the dealer-owner.

83. *Cupboard with hanging pegs and shelves. Inscribed by Stephen Alb[ie, ee, or u] s or r as painter in 1840. Found in Uxbridge area of Massachusetts. Courtesy, Joyce Harpin Charbonneau.*

7

Buy It Ratty and Leave It Alone

Great untouched objects can be found in two types of shops. The first is the shop in which the owner understands his objects and therefore their value; the second is the shop where the impecunious collector will be able to afford them. The first is better for the objects, for they will not have been mishandled; the second, while a threat to the object, is where buys can be made if the owner has not had time to "improve" it. This is the kind of dealer who will take a simple six-board chest and belt-sand it to "natural" pine. If you can capture the object, if you can abduct it before the dealer has ruined it, then you might be able to buy it at a reasonable price.

An auction of things "in the rough" is another way to acquire quality at a low price, but here you are up against the dealers who know value and will pay for it, and those seeking prey for the belt-sander. Recently, I left a bid on a simple six-board chest with powder blue paint because I could not attend the auction. The auctioneer neglected to exercise my bid so the chest went cheaply, at about half the price I said I

would pay, to a clean-it-down dealer. I traced the chest and offered the dealer a profit over the $18.00 he had paid; he said, "But I can get sixty bucks for it on the Cape, when I get that paint off." After a good New England dicker, I gave him both a profit over what he had paid and a chest that cleaning could not ruin since the object and its paint were less than interesting. Not only did I save a marvelous surface but I have an object (figure 36) that in the right market would bring much more than the $60.00 it would have brought as a "pine chest." It would be harder to sell in the present "ratty blue" state since there are fewer people who understand it this way, but fortunately this group is growing rapidly.

When I talk about maintaining early surfaces, people seem greatly relieved when I tell them that I too once ruined pieces. This relieves them of their guilt, although it fails to relieve mine. Twenty-five years ago I bought dry sinks for $12.00 and $15.00 and belt-sanded them, even digging out the putty put over the recessed nail heads. It had been put there to produce a smooth surface under the original paint! As recently as fifteen years ago, I bought a pair of simple slat backs like figure 3, broke a piece of glass to get a sharp edge as it suggests in refinishing books, scraped them down to "natural" maple, and coated them with orange shellac. When I learned that I had nothing but very new and raw maple chairs, I was fortunately able to sell them at a profit to people who like that sort of thing. But it is a difficult moment when you have to face the fact that you have been going south when you should have been heading north.

We are so conditioned by colonial *kitsch* that it takes a leap of faith not unlike a conversion to see that a grungy, tattered, cracked, and beat-up surface is marvelous. Perhaps one more story is sufficient to explain that we all have to learn what makes quality—what is "early" about an early object. Figure 84 is a simple Windsor chair that has been weathered extensively. Undoubtedly, it was outside for an extended period of its life, and during that time given its last coat of paint, which is now a powdery robin's-egg blue. Because the surface had already been deeply worn, that paint went far into crevices and interstices. The chair was found in a picker's store priced at $5.00, and I said to my wife, who had fallen in love with it, "If we buy it, will you get the paint out of the cracks, because that is going to be hell to refinish?" Well, neither of us got around to refinishing it before we discovered that what was delicious about it was its surface and paint. If this piece had been sanded (the only way to get the paint "out" and the surface smooth), there would have been nothing left but a bunch of ugly new sticks. The original idea was that when "refinished," it would be like figure 31. But it could never have looked like that since it does not and never did have that elegance of form. The parts by themselves are just not great, but as an "untouched" object it is wonderful.

84. Side chair. Probably New England. Mid-nineteenth century. Courtesy, Elizabeth D. Kirk.

85. *Top view of figure 85a.*

85a. *Card table. New England; purchased in central New Hampshire. 1790–1840. John T. Kirk.*

So much for stories that display my sins and give comfort to the guilty. A story that I find more comforting, since it occurred after the enlightenment, took place years ago when we had an apartment in New Haven that contained the few pieces we had managed to acquire while being graduate students. One of them is seen in figures 85 and 85a. Various people coming into the apartment sought to say something comforting about this ratty stuff, and the comments usually ran: "Isn't this cute," or "Isn't this interesting," or "How unusual." One day the parents of a friend came in and the wife took one look at the top in figure 85 and said, "When I see something like that I just think it should be thrown out." We felt a great sense of relief that somebody was taking it seriously, reacting to the object rather than being sweet. She had perceived what there was to see. She did not like it but that did not matter—she had said something that showed that she had looked.

The top of this card table could be pulled together so that the cracks would disappear, but that would make the cleats stick out even farther. They could be cut back and the whole thing sanded, but what would you have but a new piece of pine with new color? It is possible to say, "But this is not what the cabinetmaker made, nor what he intended; he would hate it." That is absolutely true. I am sure he would want to neaten it up, and the idea that this surface was to be published in a book would horrify him and he would not want his name associated with it. It would be possible to sand it down and reshape it to be more "like it was," then repaint it, but would that bring it nearer to its original state? Because of shrinkage and warping, we do not know *exactly* how it was. We do know that the top was as deep as the cleats are long, but we cannot make the main board deeper again except by putting in a filling piece that would look new, and give us paired narrow lines unless it were all

sanded and painted. If you begin removing original parts, shortening the cleats to line up with the main top boards, say, you are making the piece smaller than it was before—you are not taking it "back to the original." What I am saying is that there is no way to restore this piece as the cabinetmaker originally made it and that we do not know how it originally looked. If you want a clean and neat card table, make a reproduction of this and paint it. But admit that it is a copy of what you *think* the table looked like, for you can only guess at the original size and surface.

What makes this a great piece of American primitive furniture is that it has become personal, quite different from when it was originally made. It ventured forth from the shop into a home and then a series of homes, where it received a variety of treatment from people, and probably from animals and the elements as well. It became an object that had its own experiences; it became uniquely itself. There is no piece exactly like it even if it once had an exact mate; but what is an "exact mate" when you are talking about hand-made objects? It must be accepted as is. To dislike it is the same as disliking the face of T. S. Eliot or Robert Frost in very old age. This table has its history and character, and it deserves to be understood and appreciated for what it is, not for what it once was or could be made into, and if you do not like it leave it to those who do.

THE IMPORTANCE OF SETTING

Figure 86 was found in an antique shop with figure 44, and more than one person was amazed that anybody could appreciate either. What is figure 86? It is a very ratty early-eighteenth-century chest over drawer. Not only is the entire surface untouched, but the front of this chest section has large plane marks and a beautiful purple-mulberry-red paint. The drawer once had the

86. Chest over drawer. New England. 1710–1735. Privately owned.

cotter pin brasses that were popular during the William and Mary period, 1700–1735, and therefore dates from that time. It now carries the back plates of very early Queen Anne brasses, used between 1730 and 1750; they are beautiful in form and wonderful to find here. The top is worn to a rough-grained surface. All that would be sufficient to make it a piece of merit, but it also has particularly fine proportions: it is small and very shallow, which gives it verticality instead of the boxlike quality found in so many of these pieces.

Beyond that, it has been damaged and interestingly repaired. At some point in its history the front right foot got kicked out, causing that section to split away and almost come loose from the end board. It was pushed back and then held in place by a whittled rod that runs through that foot, under the drawer, and through the other end board. The rod has a knob left on its right-hand end and a nail through the left end to keep it from slipping out.

Some who saw this piece in the antique shop,

and then in the modern summer cabin full of "nicely" refinished objects where it was kept for a few weeks before being transported to its new home, thought that anyone who could appreciate such a thing was short on sense, had questionable taste, and could definitely be a bad influence on other people. When, however, they saw it in an appropriate context, figure 87, it suddenly made sense and its greatness was perceived. Seen against polished pine floors, smooth plaster walls, and glossed-up objects it said, "I am a foreigner, I am very, very different and really quite ratty." In a proper context with equally grungy floors and plaster walls, where it was close to similarly untouched objects, it was understood by the very people who had scorned it. This context was the world of which it had once been a part, but early objects do not have to be seen in "period settings." They need not be put into an early house. In figure 88 the same piece is treated as a piece of sculpture, co-existing in a room with modern pieces. There is no reason why it cannot go into such a modern context along with steel, chrome, and glass; it just cannot be in a third-rate, over-refinished "colonial" setting—but then who can and maintain any dignity? It is informative to realize that in figures 87 and 88 the chest over drawer and the rug are in almost the same position against the same wall and floor; only the incidental objects have been changed.

The spotted cupboard in figure 89 is seen in an early context and looks as though it has grown there; it seems absolutely at one with its surroundings. The rough elements of adjacent board and plaster walls, beamed ceiling with wooden boards above (all properly painted white), are like the cupboard: simple, rough rectangular surfaces. They go together, they blend into a kind. But it would perhaps be more interesting, certainly more striking, if this cupboard were put in a modern context where it would be isolated, as in figure 2, as decorative sculpture.

Much early sculpture was made for particular niches, a special place in a particular building, and now these pieces are usually seen in museums, isolated and abstracted from their original context. To really understand Michelangelo's David one should see it in its original setting in the Plaza. Yet in the isolation of a museum one sees something else. To really know a piece, it should be seen both in its original setting and when properly lit in isolation. Figure 89 not only shows that a ratty piece can look great in an early setting, but that it can hold its own with great modern art: to its right is a Frank Stella print whose diagonally grouped lines move much like the dots on the cupboard.

SURFACE QUALITY

The spotted cupboard would be barely superior to an orange crate if the paint were removed. A comparison of figures 90 and 91 shows what happens when the "restorer" and "refinisher" get hold of an object. The first was once the more interesting of the two. It has rockers, and a tin heart at the center of the top edge of the back. But look what has happened to it. The edges of the sides have been rounded and smoothed; the nick or burn in the top edge of the right-hand side, just behind where the arm starts rising to the wing, has been sanded "nice and smooth"; and the whole is smooth and glossy. It has been cleaned up, "improved," made "nice to live with." Figure 91 looks old. It is grungier, and there is a great nick out of the top edge of the back. True, this nick does disturb the arching line of that back board, but to restore the chair and clean it up would be a disaster. Now it has a soft green-gray paint in areas where this has not been worn away by quantities of children using it as a potty chair. It has a wonderful immediate surface, a strong individual personality, and is not lacking in design elements: the rear edges of

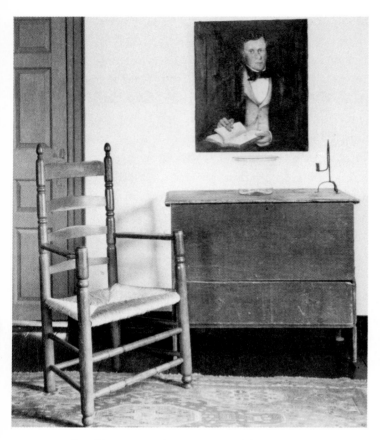

87. Chest seen also in figures 86 and 88. Chair seen also in figure 20. Glass bowl seen also in figure 6.

88. Chest seen also in figures 86 and 87. Chair, Danish, by Kaare Klint. Privately owned.

89. (right) Hanging cupboard seen also in figure 2. Slat-back arm chair at right seen also in figure 113. Brass bowl seen also in figure 104.

90. *Child's rocking arm chair. New England. Late eighteenth or early nineteenth century. Courtesy, Yale University Art Gallery; The Mabel Brady Garvan Collection.*

91. *Child's potty arm chair. New England. Late eighteenth or early nineteenth century. Privately owned.*

the sides angle down and back from the seat line to keep it from tipping backward; the bottoms of the sides are cleated. It is now much more "real" than figure 90.

The surface quality I am talking about is most easily seen on figures 85 and 126. On figure 85 the paint has worn away, and we see what should happen to pine. The softer part of the grain, the summer growth, has been worn away by the elements and by people dusting and handling it; the harder part of the grain, the stripy lines, protrude to create a corrugated surface. Such a surface is like a washboard, marvelous visually. And one should be able to touch it, for the tactile experience is like touching sculpture. In museums one should ideally be able to touch the

pieces of sculpture since their makers had tactile contact with them as a major part of the creative experience. Of course you cannot have everybody touching the objects there, for they would be worn away, which is what has happened to the foot of St. Peter in St. Peter's Cathedral—the kisses of the devout have worn away the toes. One of the delights of owning an object is that you can fully experience it.

Figure 92 was a rare early piece. It has a double, half round molding on its front, which suggests the date of 1715 to 1735. The oval escutcheon on the drawer is inappropriate since this shape was used after 1780; but it does not matter that this child's desk has an incorrect brass, for the entire surface is wrong. It is maple-esque,

92. Child's desk. New England. 1715–1735. Courtesy, Yale University Art Gallery; The Mabel Brady Garvan Collection.

with orange shellac that gives it an all-over gleam. It, of course, originally had paint covering the now glossy and glaring grain. This is now only a record that small desks, similar to larger ones, were made for children during the early years of the eighteenth century. The best thing to do would be to have a good paint faker work on it. Then it would at least have the color, and perhaps some of the surface quality, that it should.

THE NEED FOR BEAUTY

The looking glass, figure 93, is about 7¼ inches high. It is a solid piece of pine that has been dug out to receive the mirrored part, which was slid in from the top. (The mirror has lost most of its reflective silver backing.) This construction sounds very complicated but was actually simple. The center of a pine board was gouged out to a rectangle; three edges of this recess (the sides and bottom) were cut in at an angle to make a lip overlapping the glass when it was slipped in. The fourth edge, the top, was opened up so that the glass could slide in; a small board went in after it. Then, a hole was driven through the top board and the back, and either a nail was driven through that to secure it to the wall or something like a leather thong went through it to be hung over a nail. The surface of this piece is so fragile that it should only be dusted with a feather duster. Pine is very soft,

93. *Looking glass. New England. Possibly late eighteenth century. Privately owned.*

94. *Hanging box. Possibly New England. Early nineteenth century. Privately owned.*

and the paint is dry and somewhat loose. One minute of sandpaper and everything worth preserving would be gone. Obviously, it was made by someone who had no training or skill in the art of furniture making. Look at the bottom edge —it is not even cut straight. This is one of the few remaining pieces of rustic furniture made by someone whose only means of obtaining a looking glass was to make it. Not only do you want to know this piece as a friend, an intimate acquaintance, but you have to respect it as a communicator of a level of culture that most of us rarely experience or see. It is a document of a way of life. It is a record of a people who wished to have things that they felt were fine, that gave them status and self-respect, even if these objects were homemade.

Similarly, figure 94 is a record of the need of men to have artistic objects. This simple pine box has been reworked at least twice since it was made. Originally it was red, then cream with a red "chain" decoration, and then the top hole broke out and a tin patch was applied so that it could still be hung. Then it was painted white. Recently, the later white on the front board was cleaned off so that the red chain design on the cream color is again visible. It is still under the paint on the right side and back board, where it follows the line of the top curve. The box was never without conscious design, for the top edges of the sides are shaped to reverse curves and the same shape is used in forming each side of the top of the back. With each reworking it became a new visual experience.

WHEN TO REPAINT

What do you do when you find a piece that has been "refinished"? It all depends how much is left. If it has been "skinned" instead of "cleaned," perhaps it should just be forgotten. If it has been dipped in a lye bath that not only removes the paint but also eats into the surface of the wood, if it has been sanded or planed, or if any turned parts have been put back on the lathe and smoothed out with chisels, scrapers, and sandpaper, it should probably be given a decent burial. But if it has been "cleaned," that is, treated with paint remover in such a way that the wood surface has been left unabraded, and if it is not diminished in size and shape, then it is perfectly valid to repaint it. This, of course, cre-

ates for you numerous problems to be solved.

What color paint? It should be as near to the original as possible if you can find a trace of it. Even this is difficult since, just as the color of wood changes through the years, so paint colors change. If you repaint with reliable evidence you then face the problem that the piece is repainted and therefore not as acceptable to dealers or, as yet, to most collectors because this is one of the ways to hide replacements. New parts can be put into a piece, or the whole piece can be new, if you entirely repaint it.

Honest dealers are loath to repaint because they can get a reputation for selling repainted pieces, which suggests that replacements have been made before painting. Even a dealer who openly repaints a genuine unrestored piece and

95. Table. New England. 1730–1800. Courtesy, Yale University Art Gallery; The Mabel Brady Garvan Collection.

sells it as repainted cannot control what is said about the piece when some other dealer is reselling it. Another dealer might sell it as having its original paint and if it is discovered to have new paint the second dealer might shift the blame to the first. Now the first dealer will get the reputation of being a faker and trust in him will diminish. It is very tempting for a dealer to tell the truth only to those who are capable of discerning it. This makes honest, open repainting rare. But museums and collectors who do not plan to sell can repaint, and I see no reason why this should not be done if you have paid the price of a partly diminished object. It is important, however, to take many "evidence" photographs before painting to document how the piece looked when you obtained it.

The problem with repainting is just how much evidence of wear and "early" texture you "restore." The oval-top table, figure 95, now has original thin, worn paint on its top surface. The edge of the top and the base have been repainted to a rather crude black and red patterned design, which does not look old, in either its surface quality or pattern; neither is it particularly attractive, and it is hard to know what to do now. First, one should test to see what is under the new paint. It might be that someone "copied" an original pattern that is still there, although I doubt this, for anyone who had the sense to leave the top surface alone probably would not have painted the base if it had had nice paint. I would be tempted to repaint everything except the top surface in a solid color as though it had been painted over later. I would leave the top surface unpainted so that it would appear to be a "scrubbed top."

Figure 96 had its paint removed but the wood surface had not been "touched," and it still had real interest. The top arch of the lower slat was gone and a restorer was asked to put back another top so that the design would have the proper visual lift created by all three arches. Restorers, unfortunately, often think they know more than the owners. They take pride in their workmanship and endlessly run ahead of the owners, destroying objects by trying to do a "good job." Here, instead of putting back the arch, the whole slat was replaced. It was possible to recapture the part that had been removed, and it accompanies the chair; this fragment is the kind of documentation that should be kept even though it is no longer incorporated in the chair. What was used for the replaced slat was a piece of the large, broad outer band of a wool wheel. Often these can be found with the same thickness and the same curve, or they can be easily reshaped to the curve of the slats. Since they too were hand-planed and have had some wear, they are similarly and acceptably textured. This chair, then, has been helped out. Also, the paint was appropriately put back—areas showing "wear through to the wood" were left on the finials, the front faces of the back posts, the tops of the front legs, and the top surfaces of the front stretchers, where they have been worn away to a new shape by countless feet.

Figures 97 and 98 have great character which in part comes from their using twisted or warped back posts. The left back post of figure 97 warped to its present inward curve before being combined with the other pieces. This is certain, for the top slat is shorter than the bottom slat. If it had twisted after it was made, it would have pushed the whole back into a contorted shape. This oddity, instead of diminishing the chair's interest, is part of what makes it intriguing. Its black paint, which also adds to the personality, is old, for it is nicely worn, but it is not original for it covers earlier wear. The warping of the back posts of figure 98 might have occurred after it was constructed, because both have curved to the left, and the top and bottom slats are the same length; or they might have warped prior to construction and the chairmaker just went ahead and used them together. This may be a late New England chair without any ring turnings or from New Jersey, as similarly shaped slats are found in both areas. It has surprisingly elaborate finials for such a simple chair. It had been cleaned; although not over-cleaned, most of its red-brown paint was gone, so steps were taken to darken its surface. Artist's oil colors were added to a paste wax to make it a dark red-brown and this was applied in many thin coats. (It is possible to use very dark shoe polish in the same way.) The problem is that you get a surface color rather than a color that is inside the wood. This is all right when it is paint color that you are imitating, but if you mean to darken the wood itself this method is not always completely satisfactory. Also, wax tends to be glossy, but this can be minimized by applying the wax without polishing it; further use will then polish those areas which should receive wear and give you highlights in the proper places. The problem with using colored wax is that it will come off on clothing!

WHEN TO RESTORE

Warped table tops bother many people (figure 99), and it is true that this changes the design and gives a lift, a sort of flying quality, to objects that were not meant to have that design feature. The reason boards warp is that the cells on one side lose their moisture and shrink, pulling that side to a concave shape, or the cells on the other side swell and push it to a convex shape; usually the upper side is concave (figure 99). When a top is warped, it is usually taken off and an attempt made to flatten it out by adding moisture to the concave surface. This can be done by putting the concave surface face down on damp grass with the sun above, or by putting wet rags on the concave side and resting the bottom on a radiator. Such processes do straighten the board

but it is then hard to keep it that way. Sometimes iron bands are put across the bottom, but what usually happens is that cracks appear on the top surface as it dries. It is also possible to cut score marks with a circular saw into the bellied-out bottom, to remove some of the wood; the top edges of the upper surface can now be pushed down to eliminate the warp. One can, of course, plane the piece flat by taking off the raised parts, both the upward-curved edges of the concave side and the central bellied-down part of the convex side. This makes the board only about one-half of its original thickness, so you might as well put on a new board, which is often done. I ruined a good early-nineteenth-century Pennsylvania cherry dropleaf table by planing it flat. I also put a linseed oil finish on it, which is, of course, completely wrong for an early piece. It turned the cherry into a matte, dark purple.

There is another straightening process that was imparted to me practically as a sworn secret, but the teller is now dead and the process should belong to everyone. I feel about such secrets as I do about family recipes given to the daughter or daughter-in-law on completing a blood-sealed pact: things helpful to a broad audience, if they are not a source of income or an embarrassment to the teller, should belong to everybody. The process, which I have used several times, is the opposite of that usually done. It is to shrink the convex side rather than widen the concave. Put the concave side down, and on the convex side put a piece of canvas or heavy cloth so that you will not burn the wood. Then with one or two electric irons just iron the board slowly for an hour or two. Shortly after you begin, you will see moisture rising up through the cloth and the board will flatten out. (Another cabinetmaker just puts the warped board on the floor under his wood-fed iron cook stove with the convex side up, thus achieving the same thing, but not all of us have a hot stove handy.) The problem with this

96. *Side chair. New England; possibly eastern Massachusetts. 1710–1760. Privately owned.*

97. *Arm chair. New England; possibly eastern Massachusetts. 1720–1800. Privately owned.*

method is that you have to seal the side that has lost moisture so that it cannot regain it. This can be done with oil, or shellac or varnish. The few times I have straightened boards this way, I took the board past the straight till the convex side became concave and then sealed the bottom with linseed oil; as it adjusted to normal life it became straight. However, I no longer do this because I like such pieces as figures 99 and 100 with their warped tops, and sealing the bottom with something that is not original now disturbs me. It is also less work to enjoy it "as is."

Figure 99 is a bright blue table that was, when discovered, bright white. The dealer "dry scraped" it—he was able to remove the white paint with a scraper without disturbing the original blue. Had he used a paint remover the white paint would, undoubtedly, have become smeary, the blue would have been disturbed, and the whole thing would be a milky mess. I know another dealer who removed the later paint from a very great object by tapping it for days with the back of a spoon: the later paint flaked off, leaving the original. It was done so carefully that no new texture or dents were given to the old surface. There are various ways of getting off the later paint and usually each piece has to be approached somewhat differently.

The design quality of figure 99 is self-evident. Usually such square tapered legs only seem to rake sideways, for virtually all are cut away only on the inner edges (figure 105). Here the legs are not only cut to taper on the inside but the outer edges rake sideways 1½ inches. The legs have molded outer corners and a molding is used across the bottom edge of the skirt board. Surprisingly, the lipped drawer is at the end, as in a dropleaf table. This suggests that it may have been used with the narrow end coming out from the wall, in the center of the room. It may of course have been used in a more normal way with the long side against the wall and the drawer not

98. Side chair. Probably New England; possibly Connecticut. Early nineteenth century. Privately owned.

99. *Table. New England. 1790–1830.*
Privately owned.

100. *Stand. Possibly American,*
probably Canadian, 1750–1800. Courtesy,
Putnam and Smith.

visible unless it was approached from that end.

I found figure 100 in a picker's shop. The top had been covered with oilcloth; most of the cloth had been removed but a strip was still tacked around the edge. Baling wire held the legs in place, and the bottom was covered with heavy paint. It was not an attractive object except that the upper surface of the top was beautiful. It had not been repainted because the oilcloth had covered it. Although it had wonderful wear and the five pins securing it to the cleat below protruded

in a delightful manner, I bypassed it on several visits because only the top was attractive. Finally I bought it for $15.00 with the idea that the top could perhaps someday be used on something more interesting. (I still thought of doing such things!) When the remains of the oilcloth, the baling wire, and the heavy coat of paint were removed, I saw that though it is not a beautiful object it certainly is a fascinating one. The legs end in goats feet and the bottom of the central column terminates in a turned drop which is not

*101. Single-leaf gateleg table. New England.
1740–1800. Privately owned.*

unlike the acorn drops on the skirts of Queen Anne highboys and dressing tables. Goats feet are virtually unknown in America but were used in England, on the continent, and in Canada. Drops, or turnings on the base of column, are also associated with Canada (figure 132).

The picker from whom the stand was bought imported great quantities of Canadian material, so this may be Canadian. It is made of birch, a wood often associated with northeastern furniture although it was used on pieces made farther south. The legs had become loose, which was the reason for the baling wire. Often when the bottom of the central column is flat, it is possible to hold the legs from splaying by putting across it a triangular iron brace with a nail or screw into the bottom of each leg. This was done on many stands when they were made. Here the acorn prevents it, so holes were drilled through the legs to take the shaft of a screw, then a larger hole was drilled part way through the leg to take its head, making it possible to recess the screw heads.

The area above was filled and since large hand-made nails had already been used several times in the legs, the new screw holes were capped by other early hand-made nails from which most of the shaft had been removed. Yes, this is adding something that was not there, but it was seen as a way to make the object useful without detracting from it. The top has been left warped; its shape does not really affect its usefulness as the loose legs did. Recently, I faced a similar loose leg problem. I used a new wonder glue and so far it is holding.

Figure 101 is a rare form of table. It has two D-shaped pieces that form its top; one is fixed to the frame and the other drops behind as a leaf. Usually dropleaf tables have two drop leaves (figure 108). Using only one on figure 101 makes it a strong design feature: a great vertical swing repeats the horizontal swing of the top. When up, the drop leaf is held in position by a swing gate, which is not lathe turned but made of pieces with a rectangular cross-section. Sometime in its past, the unsupported front curve of the top cracked off from the main part. To hold it back in place, two huge cleats were placed under it and notches were cut in the top edge of the drawer to accommodate them. The piece was then repainted red. We know this because the red of the rest is also on the new cleats. There is sufficient wear to show that the paint has been there a long time, probably from the time of repair.

One of the ways you can tell whether paint is recent is that a new coat of paint will be inside the dents and mars of the old surface. If the paint is old, but not original it will go into the earliest dents but be missing from the recent ones. A faker who is putting on "old paint" will, of course, add "later wear"—new nicks and dents to make the paint look old. But these new dents must also be age-stained.

When this table was found, the swing gate had lost half an inch from its foot. Unfortunately, the restorer decided to use a turned part, like the feet on the four corner legs, for the extension. He thought he was being correct, but he was wrong, as the gate post, having no turned elements, never had been on a lathe. It should have been restored with a simple straight piece, with chamferred edges to carry down the line of the section above. Also, when found, the front and side stretchers had been removed, probably because an owner found them inconvenient. These were restored, for the table's design impact is dependent on horizontals and verticals playing against half rounds. The stretchers' original dimensions were known for certain because there were mortise holes giving the height and unpainted rectangles on the legs where the stretchers were missing. After replacing the stretchers, wear was faked along the top edges before and after they were painted red. It would be possible to propose restoring this table even further by removing the cleats, securing the broken front edge of the top with modern glues, and filling in the cut-out crescent shapes in the top edge of the drawer. But I would strongly advise against this, for the piece would lose some of the charm and personality gained through years of use. It now speaks its history plainly. The new stretchers are appropriate as they are needed for the design balance, which is not hampered by the presence of the cleats. Although restored stretchers should be there, the vertical lines, planer marks from a mechanical plane, should have been removed by the restorer!

Many primitive pieces have patches of iron, tin, or other material. Of course, they can obscure the design; of course, they can diminish the object aesthetically. The idea that everything that has been added is necessarily meritorious is too simple to be maintained. But the danger is that we will rip off things that might be left because we know we can "do it better than they did."

It is always tempting to do things better than they could have been done earlier. It is, for example, very difficult to get a present-day mason to rebuild an early chimney with very little mortar between the bricks. Years ago mortar was not strong and thin layers were used, since it was often the weakest part of the construction. Today's mortar can be stronger than brick; this and the fact that lots of mortar means building faster cause masons to put a great thick layer between each brick. When asked to do it the old way they invariably say, "But I can do it better than they did," a silly attitude when you are rebuilding an eighteenth-century chimney. The idea is to make it look like an eighteenth-century chimney, not "improve" it. We all have and must control the drive that says we have more knowledge and new materials and therefore can and must improve on the past. When making a reproduction it is very easy to say, "Well, let's add a few more turnings to improve what they did." What we get is something that looks like now.

The roundabout chair, figure 102, was purchased fairly recently from the Gooch family of Pickpocket Road in Exeter, New Hampshire, and although it does not have "collectable," glamorous Spanish feet it has a sweeping form rarely found in related chairs. In addition, it has an iron patch on the inner face of the arm rail. It would be perfectly possible to remove this and to secure the break with modern glues. But why bother? Why take off this hand-wrought patch which was put there as a logical solution at some date in its history? It is much like the three iron patches added to the right of the crest rail of figure 30. None of these should ever be touched.

Figure 103 is a nineteenth-century turned wooden bowl with a pink brick color on the outside. Some time ago it developed two shrinkage cracks on one side, and the simple and effective solution was to drill holes on either side of the

102. Roundabout chair. New England; found near Exeter, New Hampshire. 1700–1750. Privately owned.

103. Bowl. New England. Nineteenth century. Privately owned.

104. Bowl. Late eighteenth or early nineteenth century. European; possibly English. Seen also in figure 89. John T. Kirk.

cracks and through them loop bracing pieces of string. I have seen wire employed in the same way; sometimes iron or tin patches were used. I find all these repairs charming, personal, immediate, and revealing of earlier times when damaged things were not tossed out. It would be possible to use string or wire today, but it is very difficult to bring oneself to drill holes in an early object. We feel better about drilling angled holes through the cracks from above, putting in dowels, and then staining or painting over them. Those of us who do care about early surfaces do not like taking a step that openly intrudes into the personality of an early object. Probably this inhibition is a good thing as it helps prevent serious damage, but I do like patches on crude or simple direct objects.

The brass bowl, figure 104, is perhaps early-nineteenth-century; I recently purchased it in London and it may be English. In the shop was a similar bowl without a patched bottom. It was somewhat more expensive but what made me choose this one was the patch. Also, I liked the black scaling from countless fires on the outside. These are the things that make the bowl real, that show that it was used and eventually repaired. The patch uses a slightly pinker brass

than that of the earlier part; this and the copper rivets give a pink cast to the whole bottom. The use of different color brass for the patch was undoubtedly unconscious but the color combination of pink base, copper rivets, yellow brass sides, and black outside is fantastically dramatic.

Those who thought that the top of the card table, figures 85 and 85a, should be "thrown out" would find the top of the card table, figure 105, positively intolerable. It too once had a lift-lid but this has been removed, and the swing leg that would have supported the top leaf when open was screwed firmly into position against the back rail. When it was found in a New Hampshire shop, the dealer was considering whether to make a new leaf with similar rounded front corners to go on top—he would have faked madly so that it would have a textured patina like the present top—or whether to take the present leaf and use it as the top leaf, putting a new one under it. The only intelligent solution is to use it as is. Yes, one wishes for the greater horizontal mass of two leaves above the vertical action of the tapered legs, but there is no way to get it there without diminishing the object. So we should delight in and thoroughly enjoy what we have. It is true that this is not the way this table originally appeared, but it will never be as it once was unless you start over, so if you cannot delight in the present leaf you should ignore the piece entirely.

Figure 106 and figure 107 could each be seen as a mess. They are eighteenth-century chairs that were altered later. The first is an early slat-back arm chair, the second a bannister back. In the nineteenth century they were converted into completely over-upholstered wing chairs. The first retains on its original parts a thin coat of original black paint. Its conversion to a wing chair involved the following alterations: the rear face of the finials was cut away so that a new crest rail could be put in place, and the side faces of the finials and the back posts above the arms were notched out so that the wings could be installed. The fronts of the arms were cut away

so that the upholstery could be more neatly fitted. A curved rail was added in front of the seat to give its upholstery a curved edge. To facilitate the installation of the new top rail, the top arch of the original top slat was hacked away, and for some reason the three lower slats were replaced with similarly curved strips of oak. When recently found, the chair was upholstered. Although that has been removed, it is not the way the early-eighteenth-century maker wanted it, and it is not the way the nineteenth-century man who converted it wanted it.

So what do you do with it? It would be foolish to restore it to its eighteenth-century look: there would be new patches everywhere and you do not know the shape of the front of the arms, the three lower slats, or the top of the original top slat. If you had evidence of just how much stuf-

105. Table (top leaf missing). New England; purchased in central New Hampshire. 1790–1840. Privately owned.

106. *Arm chair. New England; possibly eastern Massachusetts. Partly 1700–1735, partly nineteenth century. Seen also in figure 135. Privately owned.*

107. *Arm chair. Probably southeastern Massachusetts or Rhode Island. Partly 1720–1800, partly nineteenth century. Privately owned.*

fing there was, you could re-upholster it to the way it was in the late nineteenth century; but there would be no reason to have an old chair done that way since a re-upholstered copy of this one, with a skirt going to the floor, would give you the same visual experience. It would be only the owners, and those they told, who would know whether there was an old or a new chair inside it. I always find it difficult to comprehend

the vast sums expended on early wing chairs where only the legs show (but that is really another subject). Just as Picasso and others took objects they found at hand or in junk yards and saw them as art, this object is being treated and enjoyed as a piece of "found sculpture." And it gives continuous amazement and amusement to those who see it and know what it is, or isn't!

In contrast, figure 107 is not particularly interesting in its present state. Too much has been done to it, and the changes have not created something interesting. It is difficult to delight in it as anything but a wreck: the finials, top of the crest rail, outer faces of the upper parts of the back posts, faces of the front posts above the seat, and parts of the arms are all gone. It was recently purchased for $10.00, and perhaps one should feel fulfilled at having bought an eighteenth-century object at that price. It now seems that the only logical and intelligent step is to put back the missing wing and to copy the padding of the upholstery that is left—in other words, return it to its wing-chair state. The problem comes when you consider what to do about the base. Do you leave it exposed so you can see some of the old chair? The remains of the cut-off pleats show that when upholstered, there was a skirt that covered the base. So, correctly returned to its upholstered state, it would have a skirt; but then you would hide the William and Mary, early-eighteenth-century turned parts. If you leave the skirt off, you do not have the nineteenth-century object; you would have an eighteenth-century turned chair below the seat, and a nineteenth-century upholstered one above, in a combination that never existed in America. Perhaps the solution is to sell it at a profit and let someone else worry about it.

Figures 108 to 110 demonstrate the problem of what to restore. Figure 108 is a painted, maple Pembroke table (a small table with two drop leaves) that now looks very much like figure 109, which carries four paper labels of Elijah and Jacob Sanderson, who worked in Salem from about 1779 to 1810.* Figure 109 combines two styles, for the base with its fluted legs continues

* Charles F. Montgomery, *American Furniture: The Federal Period* (New York: The Viking Press, 1966), no. 322.

the Chippendale style, 1755 to 1795, and the top, when the leaves are up, has four identical serpentine-shaped sides—the taste of the new Early Classical Revival period, 1790 to 1810. Using the latest feature, I must date the table with the Early Classical Revival, but in a high-style piece such a combination *suggests* that it was made early within the new style. It is mahogany, and has elegance despite the slightly wobbly, weak movement of the serpentine shapes with their thin, almost pointed corners.

The legs of figure 108 are molded instead of fluted, an idea also typical of the Chippendale period; and the top has nice movement, perhaps more aggressively shaped than that of the mahogany table. From the front and ends, the legs have the breadth visually necessary to support the big mass above; but from an angle they look slender since the inner corner has been chamferred—that is, cut away—to lighten them. It is a fine table but it has a problem. When you look down the inner chamfer, about 5 inches above the ground there is a little horizontal, rectangular area that lacks the original dark red paint, and in that a mortise hole can be seen. Obviously, something was once attached, and it seems certain that there were crossed stretchers: one ran from one corner to that diagonally opposite and a second joined the two other corners forming an X-shape, possibly somewhat like those in figure 110. Of course, there is no way of knowing exactly what shape they had, but the horizontal marks on the leg make it quite certain that they were horizontally flat. At some point they were cut away, probably when the taste for a lighter, more open design developed. Well, do you restore the stretchers? There is no evidence of how they looked unless an identical table were to be found with stretchers intact; even then, it would be difficult to know if the cabinetmaker had done the same thing on each table. However, stretchers could be put back if the other table were

108. (left) Table. New England. 1790–1810. Privately owned.

109. (below) Table. Salem, Massachusetts. Labeled by Elijah and Jacob Sanderson. 1790–1800. Courtesy, The Henry Francis du Pont Winterthur Museum.

identical in all details. But it is better and far simpler just to leave the piece as it is. The present design is acceptable and, in terms of our modern desire for openness, it is fine; unlike figure 101, stretchers are not visually essential to this table.

Figure 111 is a different case. It is a William and Mary style table that was probably made in the first half of the eighteenth century, although this style continued, as in slat backs, to the end of the century and beyond. The top has strips nailed to its side to produce a slightly raised edge, and the base flares sideward. When found, the stretchers were gone and such a table without stretchers looks like a four-legged animal slipping in all directions on ice. Although in general stretchers do serve a useful purpose on splay leg tables, to keep the legs from spreading, they are not essential to the construction of small tables. On such a table as this, however, they are imperative to complete the design by connecting the lower rectangles of the legs while repeating

the line of the rails above. They were therefore put back and such a piece should be accepted as important even with replaced stretchers, for their placement and dimension could be determined by the mortise holes and the size of the rectangle shape of the missing paint. Of course, this piece should be priced differently from a completely original one.

Many slat-back and other early chairs are now found with their legs shortened. We have already seen this done in the beginning of the nineteenth century so that rockers could be added (figure 47). Others were simply cut to bring the seats nearer to the floor, while on some the feet have rotted away on damp floors. Figures 112 and 113 are two chairs that were lowered, the first for rockers. If you want to restore the missing parts, how do you judge their height and form? On a normally proportioned chair this is not too difficult, for the heights of the stretchers from the floor were fairly standard and it is simply a question of finding and measuring a related chair

110. (below) Table. New England;
probably Newburyport,
Massachusetts. 1790–1800. Courtesy,
Israel Sack, Inc., New York City.

111. (right) Table. New England.
1720–1800. Courtesy Roger Bacon.

with its feet intact. The form of the restored parts can be left plain, without feet, but if feet are desired then the simplest form should be used since you do not know what their shape should be, unless you can copy the feet of an identical chair. Often feet repeat the form of the turnings above, and that would be a proper thing to do if there is no evidence to the contrary. This is what was done on figure 112, but since it is a large-proportioned chair it was more difficult to decide the height of the extensions. It had been cut to just below the holes for the lower front stretcher, which was missing. It was first a question of finding a chair of similar large proportions with two front stretchers. Figure 20 is just slightly smaller in scale, not quite as openly spaced, and measures 5 inches from the top of its lower front stretcher to the floor. The legs of figure 112 were restored so that the top of the lower front stretcher was 5½ inches from the floor. This places the seat rather high and makes it unusable at a dining table. One can either

accept this and use the chair elsewhere, or make it more convenient to modern use by cutting off some of the restored pieces.

Figure 113 is a different problem. Many things have happened to this chair. The second slat from the top has lost its lower bottom edge; the lowest slat is later and crudely shaped, with large gouge marks; the third slat from the top and the left arm have both been whittled from sticks and show little resemblance to their original counterparts. There may once have been hand holds on top of the front posts although this is not certain, and the bottoms of the legs have lost a great deal. The dark green paint was put there after these replacements were made. It covers them and some previous wear. This chair, however, should never be touched, never in any way changed. The slats and left arm should not be brought back to "their original state" nor the feet pieced out. It is a delightful, wonderful, and terribly "desirable" product that would fit into the collection of any lover of primitive items. It

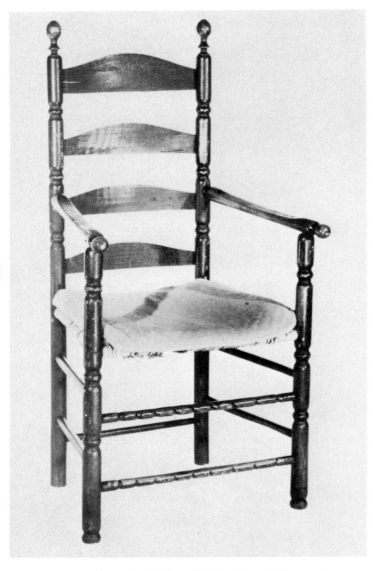

112. *Arm chair. New England; possibly northeastern Massachusetts or southern New Hampshire. 1720–1800. Privately owned.*

113. *Arm chair. New England; possibly eastern Massachusetts. 1720–1800. Seen also in figure 89. Privately owned.*

was prized by Luke Vincent Lockwood, an early collector and author, and has been greatly appreciated since. Probably it could not be afforded by the impecunious collector unless he discovered it where the owner thought it was a wreck and had no understanding of how it gained importance as it gained character.

A simple object like figure 114 needs a sense of balance. When found, the tapering point of the

left finial was missing, and if you cover it over you will realize how lopsided this made the chair. The damage did not improve it as did the changes on the preceding chair, and so the point was put back. The flat faces on the front posts are similar to those found on many small and a few large chairs. They show that the chair was laid face downward on the floor and used as a child's walker. The dark blue paint covers this,

114. *Child's high chair. New England. Late eighteenth or early nineteenth century. Privately owned.*

115. *Arm chair. New England; probably Waltham area of Massachusetts (see figure 116). 1700–1750. Courtesy, Putnam and Smith.*

but the beautifully worn top-front stretcher and the tops of the posts have received additional wear since the blue was added.

Figure 115 is shown as I found it. Look at it before you read further. I trust that your eyes have jumped to the finials and that you are saying, "They are much too small. They don't relate to the majestic crest rail. They don't terminate the fine, bold turnings below. Where is the cen-

ter split spindle? And, of course, the feet are gone!" This is a fine chair, and what one should do about the missing parts is a serious question. Not only do the crest rail and bottom rail of the back have double arching but they are bowed backwards as they move from one back post to the other. (This curvature is like that of the slats of a slat-back chair and is found on only a few bannister-back chairs.) Of course the line of

116. Arm chair. New England; probably Waltham area of Massachusetts. History of having been owned by Isaac Parker (1802–75), leader, Masonic Lodges of Waltham, Massachusetts (files Museum of Fine Arts). Gold decoration nineteenth century. Courtesy, Museum of Fine Arts, Boston.

split spindles similarly curves. Years ago the chair was upholstered from the seat up. Undoubtedly the finials were hacked off then to make a smoother line for the top of the upholstered form. The base, from the seat down, was left exposed and painted Chinese red. Seeing the base left visible when the top is upholstered makes us rush back to the bannister-back arm chair, figure 107, which we puzzled over, asking whether we could leave a base exposed below an upholstered top. The Chinese red on the base of figure 115 is evidence for what we wanted all along, an upholstered back and an open base. Although we know that figure 107 was never like that, the red is evidence that this adaptation was done on at least one chair in the nineteenth century. Now we can do it to figure 107 with some excuse.

But what do we do with figure 115, for the back is too good to cover up? First we pull out all the upholstery and other tacks. Then we see if we can get the Chinese red off without disturbing the original red-brown paint, which can be seen untouched on the upper half, where it was covered by upholstery. After removing the paint, we take off the textile that covers an early seat. We do this when the paint is gone so that the seat is not unnecessarily messed up by drops of red paint and paint remover. And then what? Well, I feel that the back has a tooth missing and that a new split turning should be made. I mind very much that the back posts do not terminate in elaborate finials, but what forms should they have? Years ago, long before I bought this chair, I saw a related one in Boston at an antique dealer's, and was so excited that I asked for a Polaroid to be taken; it is not a very good photograph but from it I know that a ball form terminates the finials. But what else? You can imagine my delight when during a recent trip to the Museum of Fine Arts in Boston, I saw their newly acquired chair, figure 116. Here is the evidence needed for the restoration of the finials.

Between the Polaroid and measured drawings of the finials of figure 116, proper finials can be concocted for figure 115, but it must be remembered that they are concocted. Perhaps in time I will come to feel that even such restorations are improper. Certainly there are those who already say so. Really an object like this should be left untouched and placed in an early rural historic house where such changed objects are appropriate. It would mean re-upholstering it though, for the changes to the finial areas result from over-upholstering it!

There are very few early authentic open shelves with or without a closed cupboard below. Many are displayed in museums, historic houses, and collections, but most of them have been seriously altered or are totally new. They have been "desirable" ever since the late nineteenth century, when collectors began seeking them for open display of their pewter, china, glass, and other small items. A completely original one would be expensive, but if the seller of figure 117 understood and admitted its altered state an impecunious collector might be able to buy it. It is untouched except that its top should be 8 to 12 inches higher in the air. This is the original top for it carries the same paint history as the rest, but it was lowered, possibly for a room with a lower ceiling or to get it out of the door—it is now just door height. The shaped board on the inner face of the sides should continue up to the top, and probably across the bottom edge of the top (there is a narrow line where the original paint is missing). What else is missing? If you look at the shape of those boards on the inner edge of the sides you can see, about halfway up, paired serpentine-shaped saw lines, which at present make no sense. Early designs make sense. The designer-makers did not just dream up decorative shapes and forms and use them in an unrelated fashion. If you could look inside the board, you would see that there is a small area

on the back which carries no original paint and there is a mortise hole in the end boards; this suggests that there was once a narrow board or rail running across, beginning and ending behind the back of those thin boards, between the paired serpentines. In fact, it was a plate rail, used for supporting plates leaned against it, their top edges facing out toward the viewer rather than resting against the wall behind. A similar rail also went across the upper opening to hold the large platters at the same angle. Also there are grooves in the shelves, grooves shaped to receive plates at that angle.

When the piece was found, it was painted with white enamel; under that was the early paint and its evidence for proper restoration. Indeed, it once had an exciting array of colors. At the time it seemed too much work for the collector to tackle the problem of carefully removing the later paint, so this was repainted with an easily removable water-base paint of a dark grungy color until the piece could have its missing parts replaced and be properly cleaned to the original paint. To get some texture to the surface, a burlap bag containing very dry, powdery earth was beaten against the surface when the paint was almost dry. The paint, taking on some of the dirt, became something like a typical early surface. One does have to worry about dusting this piece.

Figure 118 is a double-spouted pot. There is an inner lining which has a broad opening just under the hinge of the lid. Through here you can fill the lower section; the liquid from there is poured out from the side spout. The basic form is tin, but the spouts, lid, and handle are pewter. I do not know its original use—perhaps tea and hot water? Certainly, the lower part could not easily be cleaned. The upper half of the front spout is crudely patched, the handle is battered, and the side spout bent to the left. It could be cleaned to shiny tin and pewter and the dents

and repairs worked on, but I would be inclined to enjoy its present condition as part of its general freakishness.

What we have been looking at are "real" objects that present their blemishes and warts; how things were and what they have become. We have not looked at high-style pieces; their gleaming surfaces, more sophisticated in design and material, require a different, although related, approach. Primitive pieces are nearer the earth, and they evoke questions about simpler people. What were these people like and where and how did they use such pieces; what cultural setting needed to repair them and cared to do so: new tin tops on porcelain candleholders and tin handles on Chinese export jugs? (We once owned a house in Center Sandwich, New Hampshire, and one of the window panes had been broken and an odd-shaped piece of glass had been stuck over the hole with black roofing cement. Later the repairing piece was broken and yet another piece had been cemented over *it!* Is it a wonder there are more antiques found in New England houses, attics, and barns than elsewhere?) What were those times in America's past really like? And what does the continually rising interest in such pieces say about the present? These are the social historians' questions, and understanding these objects can help them find answers, but I am driven again and again to the object itself as the first question: what was it and what has it become, visually?

117. Cupboard with open shelves. American or Canadian. 1700–1735. Privately owned.

118. Two-spout pot. New England; found in central New Hampshire. Nineteenth century. Privately owned.

8

Fragments

Having explored at some length objects with interesting surfaces, many with minor to extensive alterations, it is now logical to take up the possibility that a fragment of a fine piece might be more worth owning than a complete fifth-rate or even second-rate one. Some fragments can be used much as originally intended, though many cannot. In a sense the arm chair, figure 47, is a fragment of the original arm chair. The splat is an early replacement, the rockers do not belong there, and the feet are gone; the slat-back arm chair, figure 106, is a similar fragment, but one can sit on either while treating it as found sculpture.

There are, however, items such as figure 119 that can never be of "use" to anyone except the faker. At some point, its finials were cut in half and a strip tacked above, probably to carry upholstery. Further evidence for upholstery on the upper part is the later gray paint on the bottom 6 inches of these back posts. The rest retains a wonderful surface, with much of its original red paint. This piece could be "cannibalized" with another chair that has lost its back: one could consider combining it with 120, for instance, to make a whole chair. One can start by incorporating the three split bannisters of figure 119 either with their nicely shaped lower back rail or with the simpler lower back rail of figure 120, which did house three split bannisters. The problem is that the crest rail of figure 119 is made to go between back posts and figure 120 needs one that fits on top of them. To "cannibalize" these two you would have to concoct a new crest rail for figure 120, or else modify its back posts by adding finials and fitting the crest rail below them. It would be simpler, though, to pull off the back posts of figure 120 and fit on all of figure 119, and then restore the top of the finials and the feet. This would give you a salable, and a useful, chair. Yet how much better and easier to appreciate figure 119 for what it is. At present it is hanging on a rough plastered white wall where it makes a striking impact. Instead of lamenting that most of the chair is missing, the remainder is being enjoyed. If it were a complete

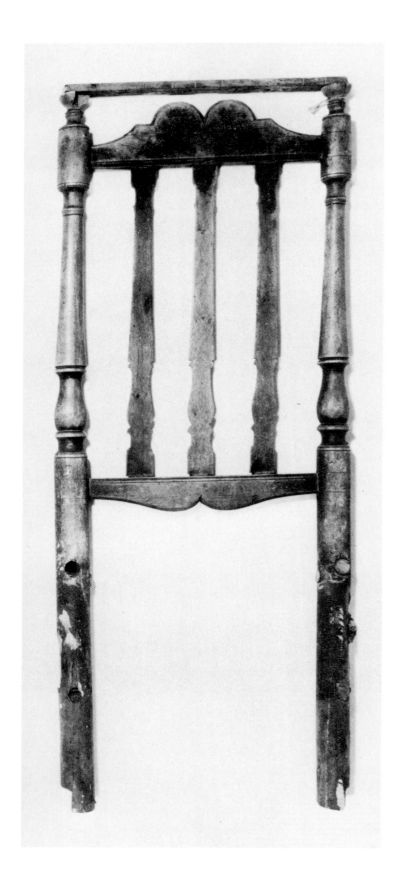

119. (left) Back of side chair. New England; probably southeastern area. 1710–1800. Privately owned.

120. (above) Remains of side chair. New England. 1730–1800. Privately owned.

121. *Arm chair. New England; possibly Connecticut. 1740–1810. Courtesy, Yale University Art Gallery; The Mabel Brady Garvan Collection.*

chair, attention would not really concentrate on the fine shape of the crest rail, the back posts, the split bannisters, and the untouched part of its surface. I think their quality justifies the heightened attention they now receive.

Figure 121 is a complete chair but compared to figure 119 it would be an embarrassment to have around, for it started as a terrible design: wobbly crest rail movement, aborted finials, and weak, over-complex turnings (particularly those on the back posts just under the arms, that meander to barrel forms). Further, it has been skinned and blessed with orange shellac. It is better to have a little first-class design than a great deal of second-rate. With the latter, you avert your eyes hoping they will land on something where they can relax and enjoy. Obviously the total chair is worth more (that is, would cost more), but it is the kind of object I continually would have to excuse to everyone: "Well, I know it's not one of the best but it was cheap." Living with some-

thing you have to find excuses for is draining.

Figure 122 shows three shelves that hold small wooden objects, most of which are fragments. The stack of three boxes with brilliant blue paint is also seen in figure 67. At the right of the center shelf is a superbly shaped, turned William and Mary leg, 1700–1735, with original brown paint. On the top and bottom shelves are two very fine bun feet; the upper one has a larger mass, the lower one a horizontal orientation. There is a New England corkscrew finial from the pediment of a meeting house in Dorchester, Massachusetts. It and a shell-like wooden scoop have been isolated in figure 123. On the top shelf is a wooden bowl that is warped so that the top edge has become a dramatic serpentine shape. The front stretcher with double baluster turnings and central ring seen on the lower shelf could be part of the group of similar stretchers seen in figure 124.

The two pieces in figure 123 have both beauty

122. Wooden objects; two also shown in figure 123. For region and dates see text. Privately owned.

123. Finial and scoop. Seen also in figure 122. Finial: from Meeting House Hill, Dorchester, Massachusetts (label on finial). Eighteenth century. Scoop: New England. Probably nineteenth century. Privately owned.

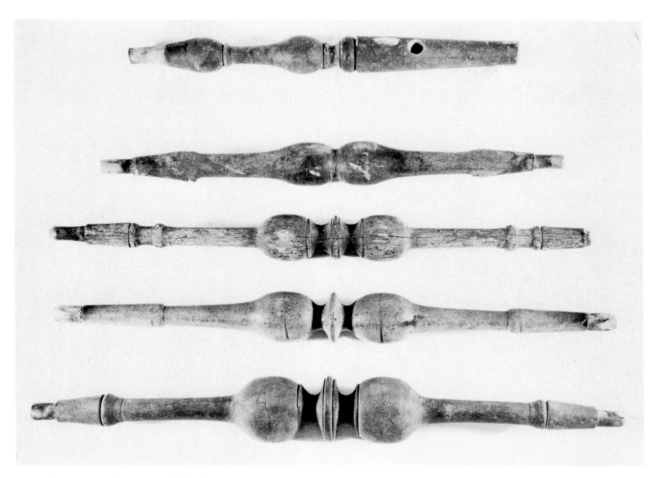

124. *Front stretchers and Windsor chair leg. Stretchers: largest from the Philip Walker estate, East Providence, Rhode Island. Third from bottom found in Mooresfield, Rhode Island. Other turnings New England. Eighteenth century. Courtesy, Knut Ek.*

125. *Side chair. New England; probably Connecticut. 1740–1800. Courtesy, Yale University Art Gallery; The Mabel Brady Garvan Collection.*

126. Panel. Connecticut; Wethersfield area. 1680–1710. Courtesy, Old Sturbridge Village.

of form and surface. The finial shows the weathered paint one wants on an untouched outside ornament. The scoop has the soft, smooth surface of something that was continually handled. Although the small break at its left interrupts the flow of line, I would not fill it in.

The front stretchers and Windsor leg in figure 124 are a grand collection of untouched forms.

Individually they are interesting, as a group they are fascinating, and each is better than figure 125, a rural attempt to use a "Queen Anne" crest rail on a bannister-back chair. Even though there is no reason why this could not have been an exciting achievement, all the parts, except the shape of the split spindles, are a disaster: the shape of the turnings of the front legs and back

*127. Chest over drawer. Modern. Courtesy, Yale
University Art Gallery.*

posts above the seat rail is poor, but not as
poor as the front stretcher, which has as much
graceful movement as a Flash Gordon raygun.
The chair now has a red glossy finish that makes
it look as if it had been dipped in liquid cherry
Jello.

Figure 126 is a panel from a late-seventeenth-
century chest or cupboard, 1680–1710, that was
made in the Wethersfield area of Connecticut.
Probably it was once in a chest similar to that
in figure 127, and it now hangs in the art gallery
of Sturbridge Village in central Massachusetts.
It is properly displayed as an art object, alone on
a white wall. It is unquestionably better than
the complete piece, figure 127, which is a total
fake.

128. Looking glass. European, probably northern. Late eighteenth century or early nineteenth century. Privately owned.

The looking glass, figure 128, was probably made in northern Europe in the eighteenth century. It is the type that has been sold throughout this century as American or proper to American rooms. A few might have found their way here soon after their time of manufacture, but most have come within the last hundred years for the antique market. Usually the decorative, reverse-painted glass edging is cracked and parts are missing. When this one was purchased, the missing parts had been replaced but they were so poorly painted, awkward in form and color, that they were removed, making it easier to enjoy what is original; your eyes do not have to constantly dodge the poorly replaced parts. Properly painted new glass could be inserted in the left side by accurately copying that which remains on the right; and the top edging could be invented by concocting from what remains. But what should you do at top center? It might be possible to copy the glass from a similar looking glass; it is also possible to enjoy what is left of the original.

Figure 129 is the top of a "tea table." It would have had a base like that on figure 95. This top has been owned for years in hopes that a great base without a top will come along. I would not attach it to a foreign base, making a "marriage"; rather, I would hang it on the wall so that it could be seen as shown. It has great form, great color—silver gray—and great surface. I would do the same with the crest rail and splat in figure 130. The movement of reverse curves in the splat is exciting and the crowning by the arched and serpentined top rail is beautiful.

Why we cannot enjoy bits and pieces, I do not understand. How many millions have stood in wonder in front of headless Greek statues or disembodied Greek hands? A good part—even if one longs for what is missing—is far better than a complete but totally boring piece.

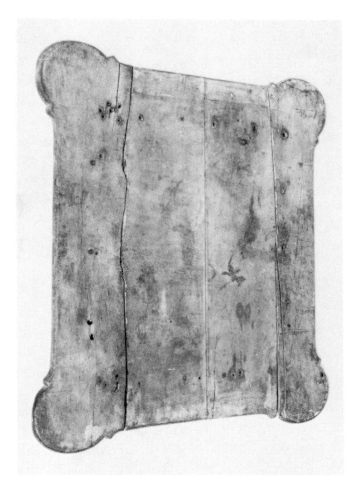

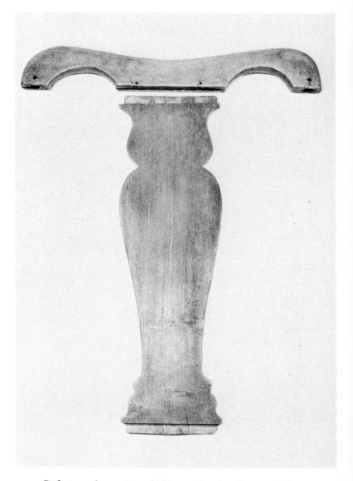

129. *Table top. New England; probably Rhode Island. 1730–1800. Courtesy, Knut Ek.*

130. *Splat and crest rail. New England; possibly Connecticut. 1730–1800. Privately owned.*

9

Shops

As has been said several times, the only way to find a good object not already discovered by someone else and priced accordingly is to go where discoveries can still be made; that is, to those places where the dealer is in ignorance of what you are looking for. It is possible to find a tiger maple and pine table, like figure 54, underneath a pile of bad art glass at a price you can afford because the dealer's expertise is in glass. Flukes happen all the time because you go where the flukes can get you. Like Winnie the Pooh says about hums: "Hums aren't things which you get, they're things which get *you*. And all you can do is to go where they can find you." But you have to know what hums look like. If you do not know what you are looking for, or what it looks like when you do see it, then of course your chances of noticing it are very small. There is a story of the minister who was sitting down to write his Sunday sermon and read in the Bible, "do not be anxious beforehand what you are to say; but say whatever is given to you in that hour," and so he closed his book and stopped thinking. The next day in the pulpit he stood and stood, waiting for the Word to arrive. Eventually he did hear a small voice which said, "Man, you're unprepared."

Recently I was telling a dealer about Meyric Rogers preparing himself when he was thinking of buying in New York stores, and she said she did the same thing before she went on a buying trip by going through the books that had good pictures of the kind of thing she hoped to find. Figures 131 to 146 represent the kind of experience that you should be seeking. It will be difficult to find shops with so many objects, but when you find something like them this is the kind of process which should be automatic.

Figure 131 shows the inside of a corrugated iron building, with four candlestands placed upside down on a pile of new wood. According to the proprietor, "They were all brought down from Canada about twenty years ago." They are all probably mid-nineteenth-century and should

131. *Interior of shed, Leonard Antiques, Inc.*

132. Four stands. Canadian. Nineteenth century.
Courtesy, Leonard Antiques, Inc.

be inexpensive unless they are being featured as eighteenth-century American. Figure 132 shows a better view of them. All four have serpentine-shaped legs but on three of them the upper hip moves out almost horizontally before it curves down; on the one at back center, the legs go down before going out, reversing the serpentine movement. Three have crossed cleats under the top that are fixed into the post; the fourth has one transverse cleat. All of them have turned posts, one of which is particularly heavy. All the posts look much like turned bed posts and many stands and tables are now made up from them and from heavy table legs. All you have to do is cut off the bottom and top, add legs and a top, and you have "an early piece." The foremost in

133. *Four stands seen also in figure* 132.

figure 132 has a broken top. All retain an early color.

Figure 133 shows another way of looking at them; now they are silhouetted dramatically to show the outline of their columns and leg movement. Here, at front left, you can see the different movement of this table's serpentine legs. Well, how do you choose? It is difficult from

photographs, for you cannot see the texture and color of the surface, nor the subtleties of the outlines. The post of the one at front right has little change between its thick and thin areas; it is just clumsy. The one at front left is perhaps more bulbous than sophisticated. The finish on the second in from the left is a brown varnish without much interest (this is the one to the

134. *Stand seen in figures 131 to 133 and 135. Canadian. 1820–1860. Privately owned.*

135. *Stand seen also in figures 131 to 134. Arm chair seen in figure 106. Candleholder. European.*

136. Table. American. Late eighteenth century. Photograph, Courtesy, E. Milby Burton.

extreme right in figure 132). That leaves us with the furthest to the rear in figure 133, the foremost in figure 132. There and in figure 134 you can see that the paint has shrunk to a mottled or freckled surface. The surface is now a deep yellow ochre mottled with yellow-brown. The main part of the shaft has an interesting angled swelling. Its quality is seen in figures 134 and 135.

The nineteenth-century shaping of the parts is revealed when you compare it with the late-eighteenth-century figure 136. Figure 134 has legs made of flat boards shaped to serpentines, while the legs of the eighteenth-century table use wider boards sculpted to rounded cabriole forms. Comparing these two tables makes us realize that the nineteenth century can be better.

137. Ek Antiques.

Figure 134 is more interesting, more unusual, and "older"—in that it has not been skinned to death. Although the eighteenth-century one now looks like an Ethan Allen special, it undoubtedly is worth more because it is earlier in form, and many people enjoy things that look like that (which, of course, is why Ethan Allen does what it does); nevertheless, figure 134 is far more

original, more interesting, and less expensive.

Much of the art of discovery lies in seeing a small part of a piece that is mostly buried and knowing, or at least hoping, that the rest is what the part suggests. Figure 137 shows part of a shop; your eye should immediately skip all the clutter and focus on one thing. Examine figure 137 now without reading further.

138. *Cupboard. Massachusetts; Rehoboth area. Eighteenth century. Courtesy, Ek Antiques.*

139. *Cupboard seen in figure 138.*

You should have seen that arched shape at the center. There are many objects surrounding it that will interest a number of collectors, but the arch should thrill them. The wood of that piece has a gray-green paint. After pulling away the obscuring objects, I found what you see as figure 138, a tall, lean cupboard that shows marks of having had a door; it is the board standing to the right. Not only is the piece gray-green, but the interior is a dark brick red. The piece is narrower across the back than across the front: the sides slant in as they move backward. It

140. Ek Antiques.

might have been made to fit into a similarly angled recess, but at some time in its history it stood free—the outer faces of the sides are painted gray-green (it was usual to leave unseen surfaces unpainted) and there are projecting nails on the left for hanging things.

Leaning the door in place—figure 139—turned a long open, vertical space into a tall vertical box with a small, strongly arched opening, with two shelves. The door was originally attached with cotter pin hinges at this height; later, it was placed one shelf higher with modern strap hinges, whose marks are still visible. Some collectors would be tempted to take the door away, to not re-attach it, so that they could show off small items on all the shelves. Such an act is barbaric. With the door in its proper place, this is a tremendously powerful piece of simple, straightforward design. It was recently found in the basement of a house in the village of Rehoboth, Massachusetts, where it was set behind various pipes that had to be moved before it could be taken out, showing not only that it had been there a very long time but also that discoveries do continue.

Figure 140 is chaos, but it is possible to see a Hitchcock-type chair to the front right, and a "Salem" rocker to the left. These could be exciting discoveries—but your eye should see something else. Can you find it?

141. *Ek Antiques.*

In lower center, against the white ground of a vertical two-by-four, and just to the left of the left front leg of the Hitchcock-type chair, is a complex baluster turning that should immediately say, "Pennsylvania eighteenth-century Windsor." It is larger in figure 141 and you can see precisely where it joins the plank seat on which rests the remainder of the chair.

Some twenty years ago, this Windsor was found in southern Rhode Island and purchased for very little since it was a "basket case," and looked as it does in figure 142. It has sat in this condition for the intervening years, not because

it is not appreciated by the owner. He simply enjoys it as the object he found and is not in a frenzy to "restore it." Just seeing this bundle of sticks should be a thrilling experience. It is dusty —with dust of about twenty years, and probably more. To touch it was to get covered with dirt, but to lay it out as in figure 143 was a must. All the pieces are there and they are beautiful. The seat is more than aged and worn—it is weathered: obviously the piece sat out in the rain and the seat gathered water, which eroded the soft grain; the central knot slipped out.

What do you do with such an object? It has

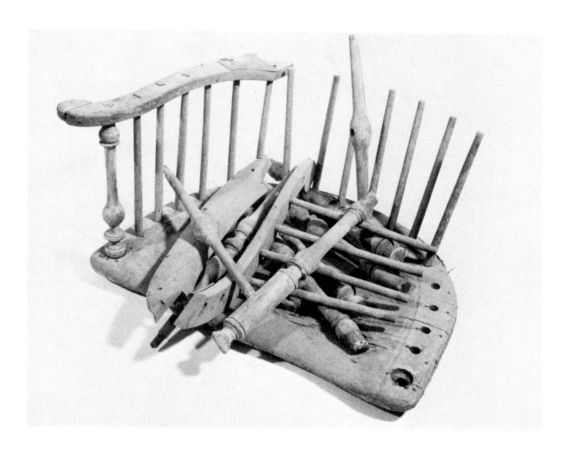

142. Arm chair. Pennsylvania type. 1750–1800. Courtesy, Ek Antiques.

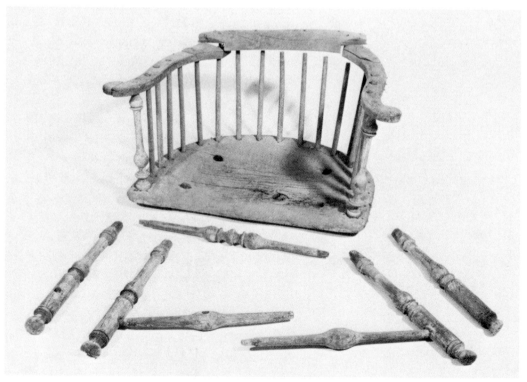

143. Arm chair seen also in figure 142.

144. Arm chair. Pennsylvania type. 1750–1800. Courtesy, Israel Sack, Inc., New York City.

superb turnings, great form. It could be reassembled to look very much like figure 144 but what would you do with the surface? Do you fill in all the crevices of the seat with putty or some filler, and then repaint it? *No.* In doing that you would remove much of what is left; you would have nothing like the original shape, and you would be looking at very new putty and very new wood. One possibility is to leave it just as you see it: either use the fragments on a wall somewhat as in figure 143 or on a table as in figure 142, and see them as interesting sculpture. If the chair is reassembled, there need be no new parts. The work should be done very carefully so that none of the glue gets on any visible part, for it would make dark, shiny spots on this weathered, dry surface. With modern glues the chair could be made strong enough to use.

Figure 145 presents much the same problem. This is a very rare and "desirable" form of X-base candlestand. It has been repaired at least once in modern times and once in early times. The early repairs were to the top, which has butterfly-shaped cleats to hold together the crack: they can be seen in figure 146. To hold together a split or crack, you can cut out a butterfly shape where the pieces touch and set in a similarly shaped piece of wood with the grain running the long way. Here, surprisingly, the butterfly cutout was filled with what looks like pewter or lead. Liquid metal was also poured through the top, around the central post, to tighten their junction. This intriguing attempt at strengthening the stand did not work. The butterflies broke and the post slipped loose. But the repairs make a good piece even more interesting. Although fake cross-base stands are made up all the time out of old parts, or old parts combined with new ones, genuine ones are scarce. This one, despite its badly wormed base and general condition, or perhaps because of this, should be purchased and

145. Stand. New England. 1700–1750. Courtesy,
Roger Bacon.

carefully repaired. The form of the feet, with the great swelling serpentine shape from the floor to the post, is particularly fine, although one of the four feet is new and has reproduction worm holes. The stand retains an early red paint which is so worn that it looks original, but as it covers the metal repairs it must have been put on after they were added. Such a piece in the hands of someone knowledgeable would be expensive even in this condition; but the art is to find and recog-

nize interesting things before anyone else does.

Part of the art of finding things is to believe that you are going to find them. Recently a research project was undertaken at Harvard University by two groups of students who were put to studying rats. Half the students were told that they had very intelligent rats and the other half that they had dumb rats. The teachers, without informing them, had given both groups of students rats of the same level of intelligence. It was noticed that the students who thought they had intelligent rats spent more time with theirs because they thought they were finding more signs of cleverness to study and report on. Their attention made their rats learn the simple skills of the tests faster. Those who thought they had less intelligent rats did not attend in the same way and their rats developed more slowly. It is necessary to believe in what you are doing, for "Unto him that hath shall be given." Dedicated buyers must be like the students who thought they had clever rats: they must be constantly aware of every possible lead, every slight suggestion of discovery. Then if they find something, they must use their knowledge and eye to decide if it was worth the struggle.

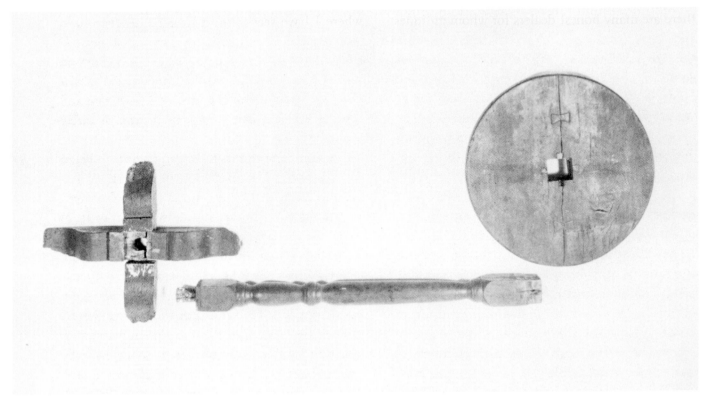

146. Stand seen also in figure 145.

10

Dealers and Auctions

DEALERS

I want to begin this chapter by stressing that there are many honest dealers for whom antiques and their handling is the chief excitement of their lives. For these people, providing genuine antiques to persons who will care for them and appreciate them is one of their major joys; many work hard to get a significant object into an important private or public collection. Many dealers have helped collectors, both those with large resources and those with little, to form interesting collections. It is easy to run down dealers, to talk about those for whom the dealing seems chiefly a means of gaining a large income or of satisfying a delight in hoodwinking the unwary. But dealers have given great pieces to important collections and they have been one of the main sources of new information about objects. They have trained countless people to see the aesthetic and historical importance of antiques, and to handle and care for them properly. Some of the earliest literature in the field of American furniture was written by dealers.

Certain dealers have provided me with more helpful information than any other source, for where I have seen hundreds of pieces they have seen thousands. There is no doubt that dealers' shops are the main places where you can see newly discovered objects. A good dealer has a continually developing source of knowledge and a training in aesthetic appreciation that is rarely seen elsewhere.

But of course the fact that one needs to begin by explaining the existence of honest dealers acknowledges that there are numerous dishonest or "partially" dishonest dealers. It is easy to make a lot of money by cannibalizing objects; by restoring part, or most, of an object and selling it as untouched; by selling totally new objects as old, foreign as American, Ohio as Connecticut, Canadian as "Upper New York State," and so on. Such practices are usually romanticized by dealers and by those collectors who know about them, but not through experience. We use the terms "hoodwinked" and "tricked" for the customers' position and "unscrupulous" as the worst for the dealers' action. We banter "fake" stories about at parties and are amused. But knowingly selling something as what it is not and making a profit is *wrong*; it is not mildly unscrupulous, it is stealing. Someday we will have laws that make auction houses accountable for their catalogue entries and dealers responsible for the accuracy of their descriptions.

The practices of the untruthful dealer carry an immense set of problems for the collector, but perhaps more annoying is the ignorant dealer, who does not even know that he is selling something with new feet or a piece that is "married." These dealers are attempting to be honest, but their objects, fed to them by other dealers, may be wrong and they do not know enough to see this. Such dealers do great harm, for a collector can easily believe them since they are telling all they know—they *are* honest. One just has to learn that they are ignorant as well.

There are also dealers who know how to be clever without being dishonest; at least not illegally so. Once I overheard from the next room a conversation between a husband and wife who are dealers. They were considering buying a matched set of eight Hitchcock chairs with original stenciling, and the wife said, "Well, we'll buy the eight and sell them as a set of six, and then later we can sell the pair separately and make more money that way." The husband's response was, "Really?" And I hope that he meant, "Can you really bring yourself to separate them in that way?" But I think he meant, "Can we really make a greater profit by doing so?" Similarly, because great American paintings are so expensive, it is possible to get as much money for one without its original frame as with it. So, sometimes the original frame is removed from its painting and the painting is sold separately for as much as it would bring with its frame. The frame can then be sold as an early one, which is "found money" for the dealer.

You should be wary of dealer's stories that are misleading even while telling the truth. Recently, a large piece was advertised as having descended in the Nicholas Brown family of Providence. It had descended in this family but only since the late nineteenth century—not from the late eighteenth century, when Nicholas himself was alive. It was a centennial piece. Like figure 147, it was made after the American Centennial of 1876, when earlier objects were openly given face lifts and entirely new ones made in the colonial style. Like most copiers and restorers today, many makers at that time felt that they could improve and add, while "being faithful" to the spirit of earlier work. This included combining ideas from numerous regions and styles.

The basic form of figure 147 is the standard Philadelphia idea of a Chippendale dressing table, 1755 to 1795. Philadelphia-inspired are the form of the case; the carving of the feet, legs, knees, and skirt; the engaged, fluted quarter columns; and the use of four drawers (the top one only looks like three). I purposefully say "inspired," for they are not identical to the earlier Philadelphia work. The use of blocked or shaped drawer fronts is associated with New England, although here the outer blocks are serpentine in form, which is a European, not an American, practice. The form of the gadrooning on the edge of the top was used in New York during the eighteenth century but not in this position. In addition to the typical "centennial" use of more than one region, there is the use of several styles. Basically it is "Chippendale," but the swags on the central blocking are an idea from the Early Classical Revival period of 1790 to 1810. This piece is late Victorian Colonial Revival and if seen as such is an exciting object. Such pieces merit the attention of collectors, but it will be hard to find such pieces sold as what they are. They should still be inexpensive, although that will soon change.

There is a shop that has for years been famous for its beds, and buyers have trudged there by the thousands. A few years ago a friend went there to buy two simple, turned mid-nineteenth-century beds with original surfaces. She was not looking for rare pieces; rather, she wanted to buy ordinary, inexpensive things made interesting by worn surfaces. She picked out two beds whose surfaces made up for their lack of distinctive form and asked their price. She was told that she could not have them unless they were refinished because part of the profit lay in refinishing them, a sound financial argument. She offered to pay the additional cost for refinishing if she could buy the items as they were. Half an hour later she left without the pieces—they were

147. *Dressing table. American. 1876–1900. Photography, Courtesy, Victoria and Albert Museum.*

not for sale unless refinished. I have since been in houses filled with beds from that shop. They look heavily refinished, like new wood. I have studied many of them and have yet to find any evidence that any part of these beds is old. It is evident from years of gathering information about this shop, and watching the many cabinet-makers who work there amidst piles of new wood, that a copy of the old bed chosen is sent to the customer. The old bed itself is not refinished at all but, at some later time, is again offered for sale. A clever way to ensure a continuing supply.

GUARANTEED AUTHENTICITY

Something that every purchaser should do is ask for a bill of sale that describes the object; the description, although it need not be lengthy, should be accurate. It should describe the piece's salient features—both its basic shape and the shape of important parts—and its finish. It should say whether the surface is original, old but not original, or new. The description should also include a date, or an approximate one, for the piece. This description should be followed by the words "Guaranteed as above," and the paper signed by the seller. Those who have never done this will be surprised at the faces of some dealers as they begin to backtrack and say, "Well, one really can't tell," or "Perhaps it's a little later than I said." Even after getting such a description and guarantee, it can be difficult to make the dealer honor it. The description should mean that you can bring back the piece if it is found to be other than described. But who is going to take your word against the dealer's? It may be necessary to get lawyers and go to court, and then you will have to get an expert who will testify against other experts. Most dealers do not want such negative publicity, but for the collector it can become a difficult, time-consuming, frustrating, and expensive process. That is why you should go to a dealer with a fine reputation, or risk only

what you can afford to, since your leverage over a dishonest dealer consists of how much you can frighten him.

Not long ago, while visiting new friends, I was asked to look at a piece of early furniture they had acquired as their one really important and expensive item. It was a small highboy, a chest of drawers on a cabriole-leg stand without drawers. This is a rare form, for usually the stand contains at least one long drawer, and more often three or four. My friends had acquired the piece from a well-known dealer who takes large ads in the most important magazines dealing with antiques. The price was $1,500 and it had been paid over a period of years at $20.00 a month. They had been told at the time of purchase that it was a rare form and that they could always return it. They had a description of what it was supposed to be. Upon investigation, however, it became clear that the piece consisted of an old upper section, with some changes, resting on an entirely new stand. In fact, the owners had felt this to be true when it was delivered to them and had written to the dealer asking if the differences between the parts did not show this. The dealer had answered that the differences resulted from the two parts having been separated for some time! I suggested that they write and say they would like to take the seller up on what he had promised when they purchased it—that it was such a rare form they could return it at any time. By return mail they received a letter saying that times were not good for antique dealers and that he could not then buy it back. Fortunately, I knew someone who had worked for this dealer and I asked him to go to the dealer and say that I lectured from Texas to Massachusetts and that I often told stories about fakes without ever naming a name, but now I was prepared to do so. The next available post brought a letter to the owners saying someone had come in asking for that form and indeed the dealer could now buy it back. The day that the piece was returned, the shop was closed, the piece was put in an outbuilding, and my friend was brought into the shop by the back door. My action was, of course, a form of blackmail, but it shows the kind of problems you can get into if you do not go to honest dealers.

A few years ago I was asked over the telephone whether I would go to New York to look at a mid-eighteenth-century piece to determine whether it had a new top. I asked what had been paid for it, and where it had been purchased. The price of $20,000 made me respond that it was much too cheap for such a piece from that shop. Since I had been recommended to the buyer by a dealer I respect and since my curiosity was aroused, I went. The top was wrong: molding changes and illogical marks made it certain, and I said so. Then I was told by the collector that two others had said the same, but each, when asked for a written and notarized statement to that effect, had backed away because of threats to their businesses. Eventually, however, the piece was returned and the money refunded. Such messy situations are frightening, but remember, it was a dealer who sent this collector for help. A good dealer can give you an immense amount of support. He or she can train you in many different ways as you come to trust each other.

THE PRICE AND HOW TO ASK ABOUT IT

Dealers are understandably as wary of customers as customers are of dealers, for customers in their turn will use dealers to get free information without any intention of buying. They do so partly for "revenge"—because they know dealers sometimes do mislead the public. Extremely annoying to the dealer is the assumption of most buyers that they can talk him down in price. Although this is often true, the purchaser need not be insulting about it. Some dealers price their

piece 10 to 20 per cent higher because other dealers assume that they can buy at a discount. Although you may not be a dealer, you may want to get a similar discount or at least a small reduction on any purchase that is not downright cheap. Attempt this, but do so without implying that the dealer is a cheat or a thief. Instead of asking, "How much will you come down?" or "What is your best price?" it is possible to use a more subtle phrase that you both understand: "Is that a firm price?" This allows the dealer to say yes or no. When I bought the bentwood chairs, figure 58, they were selected from a group of similar chairs, one of which was marked $6.50. After selecting the two chairs I said, "How much for these two?" It should have been $13.00, but the dealer asked $11.00. I replied, "I hoped you were going to say ten," and the dealer said, "Okay."

It is thus possible to avoid challenging the word of a dealer, or appearing mean, while you are finding out if his price is firm. If the dealer is firm, then either pay the price or walk away. In one of the famous shops in New York, a customer, after a long session with the proprietor, made a list of some ten or twelve pieces that he wanted and then said, "Now let's begin the wheeling and dealing." The proprietor said, "What do you mean?" The reply was, "Well, let's bargain." The customer left the shop without a single piece because the proprietor was not prepared to come down on anything. This is his right. Unfortunately, it is up to the customer to find out the approach a dealer expects.

Twenty years ago I learned to listen carefully when asking about the price of anything. I had been in Rome, where I had priced a particular style of sandal, and later I priced similar ones in Pompeii. I was told there, "I give you a special price, 5,000 lire." I said, "But in Rome they were 3,500 lire." He said, "I said a special price, not a low price." And recently in Portobello

Road, London's famous antiques-market street, I heard, "What's ya best price?" and, "For you, Sir, one pound thirty-five," and I saw a saleslady holding up a revolting twentieth-century spun pewter goblet. But what phrasing of a beautifully unrevealing sentence.

The way shops price things varies. There are those which have a standard markup, 10, 15, or 20 per cent over what they have paid. A few times if they have bought something ridiculously cheap they might add considerably more. These shops are few and far between, but many others count on a quick turnover of their stock rather than waiting for a large profit on each piece. Usually the proprietor, like any merchant, wants as much profit as is feasible. Some shops, such as the major ones in New York, must add a 100 per cent markup to cover their high costs.

It is impossible to say precisely what a piece is worth. It would depend upon its form, date, condition, and what part of the United States you are in, and even if all of these factors are the same, one dealer will still ask a different price from the next. He may have more overhead or he may have bought the piece at a different price. It is amazing to see how many pieces move from dealer to dealer, usually increasing in price as they go. Occasionally, however, a piece that has not sold will begin to go down in price. Usually this is because it is found to be different from what it purports to be, although it may be because it was once overpriced or has been over-exposed. Many collectors will not buy what has been rejected by others—which certainly shows a lack of faith in their own judgment. But even if a dealer has overpaid for a piece, because of rising prices he can generally hold it for six months or a year and at least get his money back.

You should be aware of what is called "killing a piece." This has various ramifications, but the basis is that it is often to the advantage of one dealer to diminish the reputation of another by casting aspersions upon a piece that he holds or has just sold. This is simply done. If you ask a dealer what he thinks of a piece that you have just purchased from another dealer he can permanently diminish it in your eyes by saying, "I would rather you did not ask me." This could imply that he has not seen it, or that he was upset that he was not the one who sold it to you. But the way he says it may make you think, "He knows I've bought a fake but he can't afford to disparage his competitors." Having killed your excitement and respect for your new piece and the dealer from whom you purchased it, whether the piece is genuine or not, he has you feeling that you would rather buy from him. There are other times when certain dealers, instead of saying something noncommittal but damning, say nothing at all about one of their competitors' pieces when they know it to be wrong. They can then expect this professional silence from others. You are eventually thrown back on your own judgment, knowledge, and taste, or the knowledge and expertise of someone you trust. The key, of course, is trusting. At today's prices it is possible to invest a great deal in antiques. There is a whole new group of buyers, mostly young, who are willing to pay prices for objects that twenty years ago would have been worth one-tenth of what they are now. These new collectors have not experienced the old prices, and what they pay seems to earlier collectors to be outrageous. This does not mean that the pieces are not worth it—it just means that such prices have never been asked before.

Fortunately, some of the higher prices are being put on the items with untouched surfaces; there is a new appreciation for objects in their original state. Some of the great early collectors had the same appreciation but only recently has there been a broad understanding of the importance of untouched condition. Dealers who do not specialize in, or have not in the past specialized in, untouched items used to find that they could not sell pieces that were "in the rough." They did not have the right customers and could only sell cleaned items. Today, they find that people are asking for "a primitive in its original condition," and this gives the dealer a new problem. It is harder to make a fake with an "original surface" than to make a refinished one. With the latter you can just take old boards, make up a piece, sand it to death, and put on a clear finish. To put on an "original paint" surface is more difficult than slapping on orange shellac. But the new demands also mean that those dealers who do have untouched items do not have to spend hours getting off all that "nasty" paint—not an easy process. They can simply take a nice rough piece out of a barn, put it on the floor of their antique shop, and ask their price. More pieces will be saved from destruction, but at the same time those dealers who have specialized in faking old paint surfaces are going to be able to make a good deal more money.

"EXPERTS"

Not long ago an important museum purchased what it thought was a major early piece although it was new. Because my name had been erroneously linked to the process of authenticating the piece (I had not seen it until *after* the purchase), I tracked down the maker in New England. He said he had made it with the intention of getting it into a major museum and then exposing it—out of spite for people who accused him of little knowledge. If even "experts" can be fooled, how much more likely for unsuspecting collectors to be taken.

I was once having dinner with someone who was in the process of restoring a house for which furniture of the appropriate period and area of manufacture was being purchased. After hearing a string of stories about fakes, dealers, and museum people, the owner became silent, not want-

ing to know whether the pieces purchased for the house were right or wrong. Such chosen naïveté encourages excesses. Ignoring the standards demanded in a "regular" business inspires dishonesty and contributes to the plight of others.

However unlikely it may seem, dealers and museum personnel sometimes make arrangements that affect the normal course of dealer-customer relationships. A dealer told me of a museum director who turned down a piece offered for sale to his museum over the telephone by a private individual; he did this even though he wanted it for his museum. Then he ended the conversation by suggesting that the caller might be able to sell it to a particular dealer (not my informant), whom he named. The director then called that dealer and said his museum wanted the piece. In this way, since the museum would be paying his friend the dealer, and not a private party, the dealer could give the director a kickback from the profit he made. This is hearsay evidence, but such a situation is, alas, all too possible. In another case, a recently appointed curator of an American department in a major American museum was, soon after his arrival, offered a yearly wage by a dealer to refer to that dealer all the things his department in the museum turned down. That the dealer did not in the least expect exposure says much. (The curator mentioned here has given me permission to use his name in lectures but not in print.)

With all the willful deceit on the part of so many on either side of the selling line, what can collectors do? Once when T. S. Eliot was asked, "What is your method?" he answered, "The only method is intelligence."

AUCTIONS

In earlier parts of this book, auctions have been mentioned. Here I want to discuss their hazards and how to avoid being vulnerable to them. Buying at auctions has become a passion for many people, partly because they like the excitement, partly because they want to buy a piece before the dealer gets it and adds his profit margin. Some persons think they are going to get things that are more genuine at an auction; they believe they can avoid the unscrupulous dealer. Such a notion is foolish. One should always ask: "Why is this being sold?" There are not many genuine house auctions. In a few cases, everything really is from the house where the auction is held; but it is more common that one or more dealers, or promotional people, rent an "interesting" early house and truck in some real but inadequate pieces and a judicious amount of fakes, all of which they then sell as the contents of the house. They can easily match the type of items to the style of house being used in order to give credence to the sale.

Years ago, at a country auction in front of a little white clapboard house nestled into a New England hillside, there were two chests of drawers with turned feet. They had been refinished and had new brasses. Just before the auction began, a young couple drove up in a beautiful Mercedes with an incongruous roof rack, pulled into the yard, and parked ostentatiously. The couple proceeded to bid on one of the chests of drawers but lost to another bidder. They were going much higher on a second. Horrified, I whispered to the man, "It's a highboy top." He said, "I know it," and proceeded to bid higher until he took it at an outrageous price. He was stupid. He thought that a skinned highboy top with feet added was a treasure and that what I had said was encouragement. He did not realize that his opponent in the bidding was the owner —a local super-junk-man who had himself added the feet before refinishing the piece. In fact he owned *both* pieces and had been the under bidder on the second piece and the "buyer" of the first. Since the price had not gone as high as he

wanted on the first, he simply bid it back in, to take it to be sold elsewhere. I found he had an arrangement with the auctioneer: he would not be charged if he bought the pieces back himself. The auctioneer made his percentage from the piece that rode away in prominent splendor. Arriving that way had made the couple an obvious target from the first. People who know how and what to buy try to sink into the surroundings so that those with less knowledge will not see that an expert is bidding and use that as a weapon to outbid them.

To buy at auction without knowing what you are doing is as ridiculous as to buy a piece because it was once in a famous collection, or sold in a famous sale. Recently, I went through the photographs of English furniture sold by one of the prominent European auction houses. I had a very short time to select what I wanted, English pieces related to American work, so I took anything that seemed to be of interest. Later, when I studied the photographs, it quickly became apparent that most of them were photographs of pieces that had been overly restored or had later additions, such as late-nineteenth-century carving on a seventeenth-century piece; a number of pieces seemed to be completely new.

You must know on your own what you are looking at. Do not count on the auctioneer to be the expert; some are, but many do not want too much knowledge because then they do not have to know they are telling lies when they say, "It's a wonderful piece." There are auctioneers who know that a piece is wrong since they themselves have had a hand in creating it, and they may be owners or part owners of the pieces they sell. Often, for a variety of reasons, a piece is owned by two or more people; there is less financial risk for each this way.

Part of an auctioneer's skill is the ability to amuse the audience while making people buy something they do not really want, or buy it at a price they had never considered paying and would not pay if they thought about it. It is important for you to go through the items before the auction begins, to look carefully and judge genuineness and quality of design, to then make a list of the things that interest you and put your top price against each item. Decide only then if you are going to allow yourself to get auction fever; if so, decide what amount you will, or can, go over your top price.

At a genuine New Hampshire house auction—one of the finest auctions I have ever been to, because the pieces were interesting and belonged to the house—the old codger who was the last member of the family sat on the porch and watched many of the items he had ignored or abused for years bring prices that astounded him. Others that he had prized brought very little. He had arranged for the log chains to be sold at 11:00 a.m. because some friends from the community were coming to buy them. The chains did not bring very much but other things did. One of the high points of the day was when a pair of milking stools, still caked with manure, were held up. They were just planks of wood with three legs stuck into them; there was no attempt at artistry, they were purely functional items. (One can say that artistry is unconscious and therefore these objects could contain aesthetic balance and harmony of shape. This may be true, but in this case, although the stools were not particularly ugly, they were not particularly interesting. They were in the rough —the stick legs still had bits of bark on them. Now I realize that it is just this kind of condition and this kind of almost raw human creativity that I have been discussing as potentially marvelous, but I am also saying that very few objects achieve a level of artistry that makes them important, except as artifacts of an earlier time.) When the stools were displayed, it was announced that here were "two primitives." The

bids quickly rose in price to $110 each, and then the auctioneer said, "Gorgeous on an Oriental rug," and the price jumped to $150 apiece. Needless to say, the face of the codger on the porch showed amazement, and he probably thought, "Why didn't I spend another fifteen minutes making two or three more?"

The amount of money an auctioneer will make is in direct proportion to his skill in raising prices. He usually gets 20 per cent of what he takes in. The auctioneer is skilled, if he is any good at all, in making you feel that you want the piece, and he may make you feel guilty in front of other members of the audience for not paying the price he is asking. I remember seeing a large, but not terribly glamorous, Chinese export bowl auctioned, and one of the two high bidders was an exquisitely dressed teen-age boy. The price had reached $900 and the auctioneer, looking at the youth, said, "Well, wouldn't ya just love to have that on your dresser at school and be able to say ya paid a thousand bucks for it?" The lad bid $1,000. The auctioneer had not only given him a vision of himself in the future with a story to tell, but had made it so the boy would feel guilty for falling short of his own pretensions.

I want to stress that it is essential to inspect items before the auction begins. Great auction houses can have special lighting so that objects can be made to appear better than they are; also, small and many large defects will not show from a distance. Often when a piece is held up for sale, anything glaringly wrong will not be shown or described. Figure 148 was purchased at auction without inspection. It was held up and only $15.00 was offered. I bid $20.00 and got it. I saw that it was a late-eighteenth-century New England maple dropleaf table with molded squared legs in the Chippendale style, retaining much of its original red paint. What I did not notice was that 2½ inches had been cut off the right end of the top and leaves. This was done long ago, for

148. Table. New England. 1760–1800. Courtesy,
Elizabeth D. Kirk.

although the new cut is rough it has age color and wear. It may have been cut to fit into a narrow space. Obviously others in the audience who might have bid had noticed its state; I was silly, in fact stupid, to bid on something I had not looked at closely. Fortunately, it turned out to be sufficiently interesting in this state, for it has nice legs and the surface quality is fine—early red paint on the base and wonderful wear on the top. I could say I was a clever buyer, but in fact I was lucky to get something good out of ignorance and a truly foolish action. Of course, this table should never be restored to its full length.

Each sale is different. It is often better to let other people exhaust themselves bidding as long as they are way below your top price, and then when one person feels victory after battling to the highest bid and the auctioneer is about to drop the gavel, begin the whole process again yourself. You may have an exhausted victim stretched beyond his limits. Another tactic is to offer a high price compared to what the auctioneer is asking. Others may not want to get into the fray. Still another way is to make the auctioneer go up by as small increments as he will allow. You can outsmart yourself, however, and lose a piece by waiting too long or by not assessing the audience, your opponent, and the auctioneer correctly. If you tease the auctioneer too much, he may be glad to help someone else get the things. He has been there many times before and he will know your game. But if you play it in the right way, he will appreciate your skill. I have heard an auctioneer say to someone who was clever but not ostentatious or nasty, "You pulled that one off." Sometimes a set of things will be sold off individually and after the first is sold, the top bidder has a chance to select how many pieces he wants at that particular price. If he leaves any, they are put up and bid again. I once saw three plates going under these conditions. The top bid was $5,000 per plate and the buyer selected two, leaving a cracked one to be re-auctioned. Then he bought it for $3,000. This is correct and clever buying, and it can be done on inexpensive items.

Something that the unwary should know about is the "ring." This is the process by which a group of dealers (private citizens can also be invited to take part) agree to work together at an auction; they do not then bid against each other. One member of the ring acquires the pieces they all want without competition from other members. After the auction, the members hold their own auction of the pieces the ring has acquired and financial adjustments are made to all members. This can mean that the original seller loses a great deal of money. A ring is immoral and in some places illegal, but it is difficult for an auctioneer to prove one is at work, and it is extremely hard to break it up. A good auctioneer knows who is in the audience, knows the particular kind of item they buy, and if they are not bidding on the things they collect or stock he realizes what is going on. But he cannot make them bid. Theoretically, a ring can be an advantage to others in the audience, for members of the ring are not trying to outdo each other by going beyond what they would normally pay. But it can be that the ring decides to "get" a member of the audience whom they invited into the ring and who refused, or whom they simply dislike, by forcing up the prices on a given piece beyond its value. With the adjustment of prices in their own auction,

each will lose very little if they have not been able to stick it on the one they are trying to "get."

If you have a reputation as a big spender or as someone who really knows authenticity and quality, it is important that others in the audience do not realize *you* are bidding, because those with less-felt certainty and those who respect your reputation will follow your lead. Some people bid by just lifting a pencil or holding a program at chest level, and it is marvelous to see this kind of subtle bidding at the great auction houses. It is possible to arrange with one of the auction personnel who is scanning the audience for bids that you will be bidding on a particular piece as long as you hold your program up, or sideways, or down, or as long as you are or are not looking at him. It is also possible, however, to be too clever and waste time making these arrangements when no one cares whether you are buying or not. Usually, too much preparation makes it all too complex.

After a local auction is well along, you can sometimes ask one of the personnel if they will put up a specific piece or two. They may not want to do so because they know that certain kinds of pieces sell better at certain times of the day; or they may know that a person who wants that particular piece is coming later. But often they are willing to put up your request in the next fifteen minutes or so. I recently saw someone ask for a set of wooden bowls with wonderful colors to be put up, but the auction personnel brought out the wrong set; these bowls were cracked and lacked paint. The person who had made the request was embarrassed not to bid and bought them when he did not want them. Whether this was an intentional switch on the part of the auctioneer's staff is impossible to say, but just as one should forthrightly protest against badly cooked food or chilled red wine in restaurants, so one should stand firm at auctions because, theoretically at least, they are there for you.

11

Quiz Yourself

After public lecture series and university courses I give a quiz designed to focus what I have been trying to teach. I find that these quizzes make several things evident to the participants. First, that specific, factual knowledge is essential to any real comprehension of American furniture and other objects: that knowing when each form of molding, foot, turning, etc., first appeared, and how long it remained popular in each area of manufacture, is basic in understanding what features might be present on a piece from a given time and place. Second, such quizzes show that it is imperative to understand the visual impact of a period, a time, a style, since any moment in the past focused—and was focused by—its visual demands.

I also give quizzes since most people think that after attending ten or so lecture-discussions they are ready to charge out and invest—risk—their savings. They need to find out just how much they do know and how much they do not. Everyone should realize just what tools he has for evaluating a piece, whether it is in a shop or at an auction, in a museum or a private collection. A quiz has also helped many people realize what kind of reading and looking they need to do.

This chapter is here for the same reasons. Figures 149 to 160 are all unusual in some way; they stand outside what is ordinarily expected of their form or type, or they have some problematic or interesting feature. Figures 157 to 160 are two pairs; one of each is a copy of the accompanying piece. Each piece is approached in three stages. First, there are photographs of the objects themselves with essential questions that you should automatically ask yourself. Then follows an extended list of questions. These are some of the questions you should have asked yourself in responding to the first set. Last comes a section in which the objects are identified, and commented on.

FIRST QUESTIONS

Figure 149: Which of the two outdoor latches is older and why?

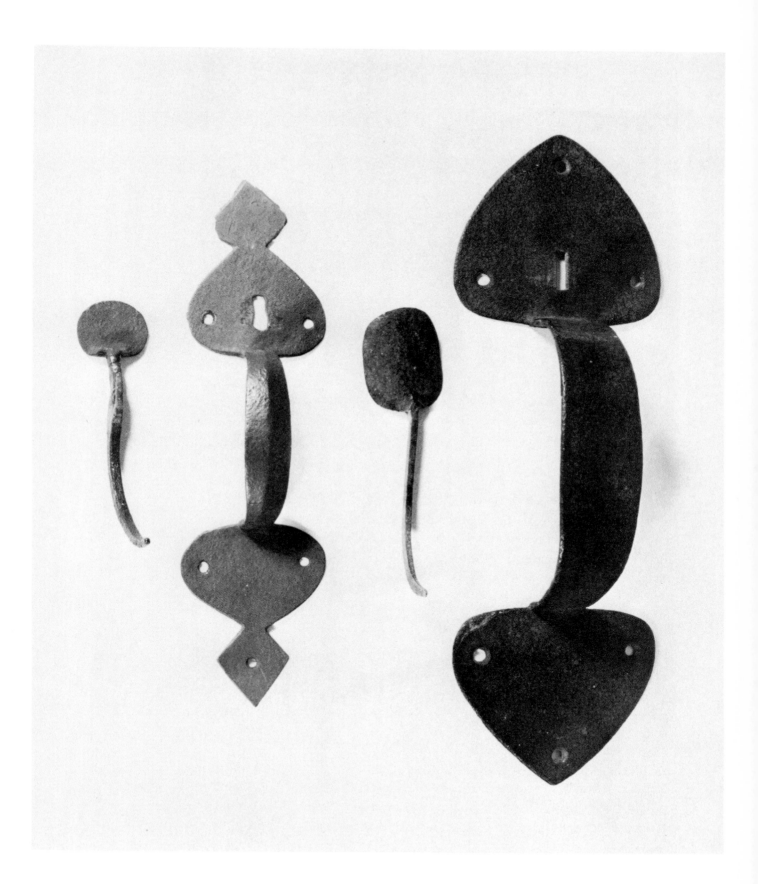

Figure 150: When was it made?

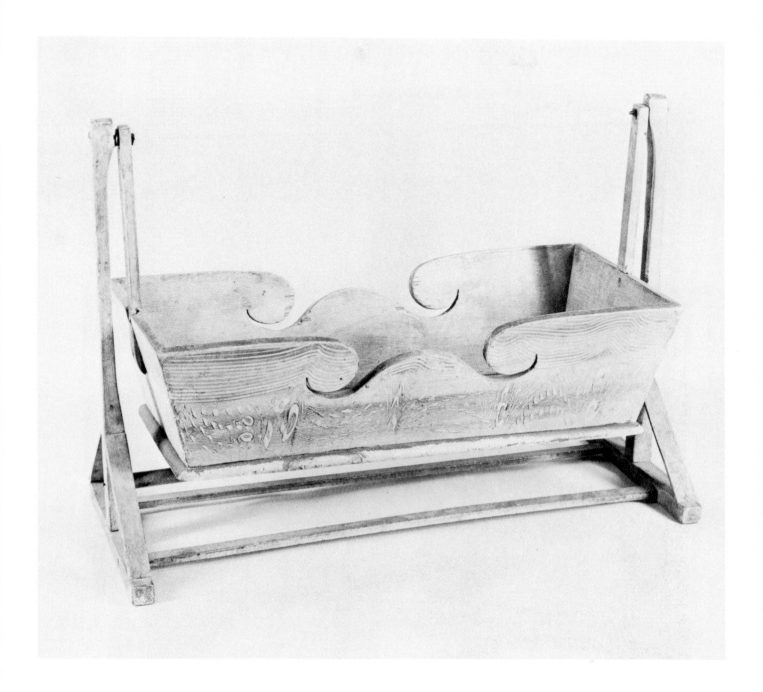

Figure 151: When was it made?

Figure 152: When was it made?

Figure 153:
Where was it made?

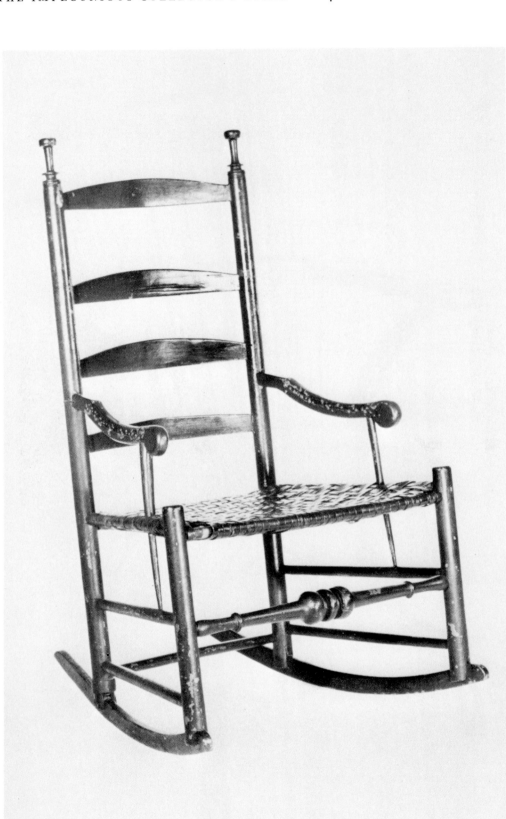

Figure 154: When and where was it made? What about the rockers?

Figure 155: Realizing that it is difficult to say
from the photograph, are all the parts original?

Figure 156: What parts
are replaced and what
part repaired?

Figures 157 and 158: Which box is a copy of the other?

Figures 159 and 160: Which table is a copy of the other?

SECOND QUESTIONS

Figure 149: What do the all-over forms suggest? Do the shapes of any details suggest dates?

Figure 150: What are the different styles and features incorporated in this chair? What is their chronological sequence?

Figure 151: What date is the large-scale movement of the shaping of the board sides? What kind of wood grain is the painted decoration imitating? What does this suggest?

Figure 152: How does it differ from figures 33, 34, 35, 38, and 86? The feet, the cockbeading around the drawer, the brasses, and the drop in the center of the skirt rail should all be taken into consideration.

Figure 153: Is the shaping of the legs similar to that of the Windsor chairs previously discussed?

Figure 154: What does the use of plain, non-ring-turned back and front posts imply? Does it help to date and regionalize the piece? How do you know if the rockers are original?

Figure 155: How about the differences between the front stretchers? The side stretchers? What about the holes in the front left leg of the chair at the right? The feet? The seats? The paint?

Figure 156: What parts are most likely to have needed replacement after extensive use? Would each new section have to be a complete unit? If not, where would the attachment be?

Figures 157 and 158: Which one has harder edges and more *obvious* wear?

Figures 159 and 160: Which table has the more exciting movement to its legs? The top of figure 159 has expanded, causing gaps to appear between the pieces of applied edge molding (one gap is over the right front leg); the top of figure 160 has shrunk, pulling the joints of its molding tight together, even pulling away from it in some places. What do you know about wood shrinkage and expansion?

COMMENTS

Figure 149: Latches. John T. Kirk.

For years I have owned the larger latch on the right. Many people, amazed at its size, have said, "It must be very early." I have always replied, "It *looks* very late-nineteenth-century to me," but I had never taken time to find evidence for what was somehow visually apparent. The almost heart-shaped ends just seemed too rounded, too full-blown, too Victorian to be early. I knew that Shakers, and others, had made iron latches late in the nineteenth century and thought that this might be one of them. Then one day the umpteenth person said, "Oh look at that early latch," and I said, without thinking it out, "Oh, no, it's late. Look at"—and while speaking, I *saw* for the first time—"the holes in the ends. Not only are they large; they're bevelled for the tapered heads of screws." Early latches were secured by nails driven through small holes, as in the one at the left, and cleated over on the inner side of the door. The one on the left has the active, dramatic, sharp changes expected of eighteenth- and early-nineteenth-century forms. That on the right, although beautiful, is incapable of this kind of visual impact: comparatively its form sludges its way about. It is possible to date the larger one both by its allover visual feel and by specific evidence.

Figure 150: Side chair. Privately owned.

Various authors have called similar chairs "bannister backs," or "Carver types." This is neither. As discussed under figure 42 the basic form of this chair's front legs, front stretcher, and back posts is that of a bannister-back chair (figure 121). The crest rail, with ears, is Chippendale in style (figure 43). The spokes of the back are Windsor in idea. So far the crest rail is the latest feature, 1755–1795, although Windsor spokes are dateless, beginning around 1740. But what about the front feet? Where have you seen them? They are on the mid-nineteenth-century tables, figures 54, 56, and 57, and the "Hitchcock" chair base in figures 140 and 141 uses the same idea. It is a button foot with an in-curving shape above. Such a foot is often found on simple tables and stands and is often incorrectly termed a "country Queen Anne foot." Another late feature is the use of very thin rings on the front legs. Usually, by the nineteenth century, ring turnings had disappeared. Here they are preserved in a chair that demonstrates the continuing impact of the William and Mary taste that began in America about 1700. As Benno Forman has said, "William and Mary is not a period but a style." It knows no fixed terminal date.

Figure 151: Baby's swinging cradle. Courtesy, Shelburne Museum, Inc.

The base of the cradle is inscribed by Martin Linfield of Braintree, Vermont, as made in 1875. This may at first seem a late date for painted decoration, but it has nearly always been with us. The wood it imitates is oak; that should date it, for only in the late nineteenth century did oak *grain* become fashionable. The "flecks" on the lower edge of the side are typical of how oak grain was presented during the Golden Oak period. At other times the grain was quiet and usually painted over.

161. Chest of drawers. For discussion see text of figure 152. Courtesy, Yale University Art Gallery; The Mabel Brady Garvan Collection.

The curved line of the sides is like the loose movement found in the shaping of similarly dated bed headboards, and it is like the open movement of the large latch, figure 149.

Figure 152: Chest over drawer. Courtesy, Joyce Harpin Charbonneau.

Figure 38 is the only piece from that list of figures, p. 168, that has similar front feet. Having front boards, they reflect the shape of bracket feet that began in the second quarter of the eighteenth century. But they are also found on figure 61, which is nineteenth-century. The cockbeading around the drawer was first used in the William and Mary period to be discarded in favor of lip drawers from about 1740 to 1780, when it reappeared. When drawers were veneered, cockbeading was attached to the drawer to protect the edge of the veneer (figure 161); when veneer was not used, it was attached either to the drawer or on the case around it. The oval form of the brass escutcheon at the top is 1790 to 1810 (figure 50), but is found later on rural pieces; the round pulls on the drawer suggest a date of 1810 to 1830. The central drop on the front skirt and the narrowing downward movement of the feet are also seen on figure 161, which was made between 1790 and 1810, probably in Portsmouth, New Hampshire, but possibly in Boston. Figure 152 is a rural early-nineteenth-century echo of such high-style pieces.

Figure 153: Arm chair. Photograph, Courtesy, Victoria and Albert Museum.

The movement of the legs is unlike that of any American Windsor shown in this book; it is closely related, though reversed end for end, to the leg movement of the English chair, figure 29. The congestion of heavy parts is like that of the English chair, figure 11. It is an English piece. Usually, the upper half of an American Windsor leg (when it is earlier than bamboo shaping) is baluster-shaped above a reel, and the lower half tapers (figure 26); or it may be straight-turned above a reel and baluster foot (figure 144). The C-shape arm supports are found on some American Windsors but they are more common in England.

The metal plaque on figure 153 reads: "This being one of the Cabin Chairs which was / on board His Majesty's Ship "Resolution," / Capt. James Cook, / on his last Voyage round the World. . . ." It is displayed in Trinity House, Hull, England.

Figure 154: Arm chair. Privately owned.

Plain-turned posts mean late New England or Pennsylvania area. But Pennsylvania area slat backs have tapered back posts that usually end in acorn finials, and their front legs normally include a baluster turning and reel- and ring-turned feet. Their slats are serpentine-shaped, usually on both upper and lower edges (figure 25). Nineteenth-century New England back posts are plain-turned and use a variety of finials. This chair was found in Center Sandwich, New Hampshire, but this certainly does not prove that it was made there. Probably it is from northern New England, New Hampshire or Vermont. The rockers are original; they have the same paint history as the rest of the chair. This and a related chair, probably by the same turner, have finials that

are pieced on, that is, turned separately and attached. I hesitate to say this, for these are the only chairs where I have seen this done without its being the work of a restorer or a faker. On these two arm chairs the finials are separate pieces from the *center* of the lower reel. A faker would normally use a less obvious place. The finials have the same paint histories as their respective chairs. It must have been felt necessary to turn a separate piece when making such an extended thin neck in the finial.

Figure 155: Three side chairs. John T. Kirk.

These three chairs are primitive Queen Anne in form (figure 48), and were made between 1740 and 1800, probably in Connecticut. The chair on the right is the most battered, although it is the only one to retain a beautifully worn original seat. It has lost its feet and has new holes that go through the left front and rear legs. This was done when new left side stretchers were fitted. These new stretchers can be seen to be thinner than those on the right side; they have been crudely shaped, probably with a spoke shave on a drawknife. They have never been painted but are a beautiful old color which blends with the other surfaces of the chair where its original red paint is completely worn away. The right side stretchers are seen to be original, by their retention of red paint, even though they are the thickest of any in these three chairs. But this thickness is in correct visual proportion to the front legs and back posts, which are also thicker than those of the other chairs.

When I discovered these chairs in a picker's shop in New Haven it was possible to see the changes to the one at the right, but the other two had been "done up" to Victorian taste and were painted black with gold lining, had pansies painted on their splats, and had seats made of small velvet triangles of various colors. They had received little wear since their redecoration, probably being always in the "best parlor." Even with the later paint you could see that the center chair had lost the lower parts of its feet; the rear stretcher was dowel-like while those in the other chairs were thicker and swelling; the left side stretchers are similarly dowel-like (its right side stretchers cannot be seen in the photograph but they do have the slight swelling). The left chair has a different front stretcher. It is, however, more consistent with what we have come to expect than the other two, with their looser movement of line.

As soon as I got them home, I removed the Victorian seats and preserved them, and I tested a small area on the *back* of a leg with paint remover. (Usually one *wants* to start cleaning the most important part. But if you do and then decide to stop, you've had it.) I used a paint remover that is supposed to lift only the later oil-based paint while preserving the original. It did not even loosen the original coat and make it smeary as often happens, so I went ahead. Since the chairs had been repainted years ago, much of their original red remained, while the un-repainted chair, at the right, had nearly all of its paint worn away.

When the red paint on the center chair was examined, it became obvious that the left side and back stretcher (the three dowel-like members) were restored: they had no red paint, and their surfaces retained more of the later black paint (the other parts had had their grain filled with red paint). The front stretchers of the left and center chairs retain much of their original red paint; the front stretcher of the right chair, which is like that of the center chair, has some of its red paint, and all three are beautifully worn. So, all the front stretchers are accepted as original.

These three chairs seem to be the work of the same man. Everything you see in the photograph is original, except for the following restorations: the seats of the left and center chairs; the left side and the back stretchers of the center chair; and the left side stretchers of the right chair.

Figure 156: Arm chair. Privately owned.

Legs are the parts most likely to have received damage. They are often cut to lower the chair or in adding rockers. When putting them back, it is the practice not simply to extend them from what is left but to go up to a visual break in the design where the joint can be hidden. Since all buyers will, or should, look at a lower ring or reel for a new joint, some fakers will add new parts farther up than they need to, perhaps above the reel or even the baluster turning. On the left front leg of this chair, you can see that the tapered lower part is offset slightly to the right of the ring turning above it. The top edge of the taper on all four legs shows a hard edge; all four have new parts pieced on from this point. This raises the question, How about the stretchers? If the chair had lost most of its taper, the stretchers may also be new. Here they seem original—they have the same wear and color as the rest of the chair. They might, however, be from another chair. I *know* they are original for I saw the chair before and after the restoration and they were the same each time.

The center of the bowed top rail has an interruption in its circular movement. A part 4½ inches long over the central spoke is new, filling in what was a serious break. The restorer did not manage to achieve the same curving motion, nor the same color as the original part.

Figure 157: Box. Privately owned.
Figure 158: Box. Courtesy, Mr. and Mrs. Dick Benjamin.

Figure 157 is the old box. It is nineteenth-century and is painted a medium green. Figure

158 was made as a copy of it. When they were first shown to a class, during a test, all but one person had trouble telling the difference, for figure 158 has been painted several times and each coat, as it dries, has been treated with a blow torch and the bubbles scraped off before applying the next layer. Only one student was smart enough to smell the two pieces and then found she could detect the new paint on figure 158. There is a standing joke that at antique shows the booth of one of the famous dealers in primitive furniture can be located merely by the smell of new paint. I saw this dealer display at the Boston antique show a wonderful early slat-back chair with original green paint; later the same chair was displayed at the Philadelphia show with "original" red paint, which exuded a new paint smell. I asked why in God's name the beautiful moss green had been removed and red added, and was told, "Red sells better."

The wire bale of figure 158 is from a piece of corroded wire fencing. The problem is that the ends are still bright where they were cut, and the staple-like wires that hold it to the top are equally shiny. The shine could be removed with acid. Also faultable are the areas where the paint has been worn to the wood, for they appear a bit raw and show a *stained* pine surface; exposed areas of wood on figure 157 show a beautiful deep, rich natural color. On close inspection, the nicks and mars on figure 158 look artificial when compared with those on figure 157, and they tend to be under the paint because it is easier to make mars look old by putting paint over them. Mars and nicks put in after the new paint often look new.

The most recent method of faking "old paint" that I have heard described was probably used on figure 47. After a fresh coat of paint has dried, an area of the object is soaked with a mixture of alcohol, shellac, and a dark brown color and it is immediately lit. The burning crackles the paint, darkens and "ages" it. When in a heated state

places can be rubbed through to the wood. The process is done area by area for you must work fast, before the alcohol evaporates. The newness of the paint on figure 47 is detectable: the bottom of the front stretcher is bright green while the rest is darkened. Such an area should now be the darkest since it is rarely touched, but on this stretcher it is vivid green. Obviously the alcohol applier, working fast, missed this crucial and telling part. The upper left of the back has a scorched look. Such aging of paint is legitimate only when it is properly recorded.

Figure 159: Table. Privately owned.
Figure 160: Table. Courtesy, The Henry Francis du Pont Winterthur Museum.

The table shown in figure 159 was recently made from a photograph of figure 160, which is a grand, New England mid-eighteenth-century Queen Anne table, of unusual form. The eight-sided top plays delightfully against the square base. The leg movement of figure 159 lacks the excitement and variations found in the legs of the original; it makes the legs heavy and obvious: they have hard edges that run down into the feet. The top was made of wood that was too dry for normal conditions; as it adjusted after being made, it expanded rather than shrank in the normal way. The pins that hold on the top and secure the tenons of the skirt rails have faceted tops; they should be flatter, with only slightly rounded top surfaces, for on old tables they would originally have been smoothed level with their adjacent surface. Years of shrinkage of the surrounding board would make them protrude, since they use grain going at a right angle to the boards. Then years of dusting would have given a slight dome to the protruding part, figure 160. The pins on the copy were left sticking out and then chiseled to facets to make them "look old"; the attempt has not succeeded.

I hope you went far beyond the questions I suggested as you looked at the pieces included in this chapter, that your mind danced back and forth over what was shown earlier and over actual pieces you have seen. Any creative collector, impecunious or not, needs eventually to build a mental file of pieces and his reactions to them. You should be able to say that a piece is like, or related to, one in Nutting, or Lockwood, or any of the other standard works. But from the beginning there can be, and should be, a direct contact between you and the object, you perceiving it, and asking of it these and other questions.

We all want help, guidance, and confirmation, and although these are available, even those who spend their lives working with objects in a scholarly way are confronted again and again with things that worry them but which they have to leave as questions that return and nag at the conscious and unconscious. We must turn from everything peripheral to hold fast to the object itself. Sometimes we see there a cabinetmaker's label and breathe deeply, thinking "At last an outside 'fact,'" but how did it get there? When and why? And even if it was put there at, or near, the time of manufacture, who put in there? The maker? The seller? The repairer? I have written about this problem elsewhere (*American Chairs: Queen Anne and Chippendale* [New York: Knopf, 1972], pp. 12–14), mentioning two Duncan Phyfe (New York) labels that have been on early-nineteenth-century Salem, Massachusetts, pieces since just after they were made. So even "genuine" labels, not to mention scribbled names, initials, stamps, or brands, are not to be fully trusted without support. So, where are we to turn? To the object itself: the details, the total impact, and we confront it trained to a fever pitch.

References
and Index

Correspondence of Plates and Text

A listing of all pages on which each figure is discussed.

Index

The index indicates page references by roman type. Figure numbers and their captions are indicated by **bold face type.**

American furniture is indexed to town and state when known, and to region when a more general regionalization is necessary. Non-American furniture is indexed to its country. Only chairs are subdivided into region and form.

Only the most informative figures are listed with a text reference. Additional figures may be suggested by the text. The Correspondence of Plates and Text, pages 177-8, lists where those figures are discussed.

An indexed item often occurs more than once on a cited page.

A Note About the Author

John T. Kirk is a native of West Chester, Pennsylvania, and a graduate of George School and Earlham College. In addition to taking an M.A. in art history from Yale University, he studied cabinetmaking at the School for American Craftsmen, Rochester, New York, and furniture design at the Royal Danish Academy of Fine Arts, Copenhagen. He has been Assistant Curator for the Garvan Collection, Yale University Art Gallery; Consultant Curator for the Pendleton House, the Rhode Island School of Design; Director of the Rhode Island Historical Society; and Research Associate of the Fogg Art Museum, Harvard University. He is currently Professor of Fine Arts at Boston University. Mr. Kirk is the author of *Connecticut Furniture, Seventeenth and Eighteenth Centuries* (1967), *Early American Furniture* (1970, 1974), and *American Chairs: Queen Anne and Chippendale* (1972).

A Note on the Type

The text of this book was set in Electra, a Linotype face designed by W. A. Dwiggins (1880–1956), who was responsible for so much that is good in contemporary book design. Although much of his early work was in advertising and he was the author of the standard volume *Layout in Advertising*, Mr. Dwiggins later devoted his prolific talents to book typography and type design and worked with great distinction in both fields.

Electra cannot be classified as either modern or old-style. It is not based on any historical model, nor does it echo a particular period or style. It avoids the extreme contrast between thick and thin elements that marks most modern faces and attempts to give a feeling of fluidity, power, and speed.

This book was composed by The Maryland Linotype Composition Company, Baltimore, Maryland, and printed and bound by Murray Printing Company, Forge Village, Massachusetts.

The book was designed by Earl Tidwell.